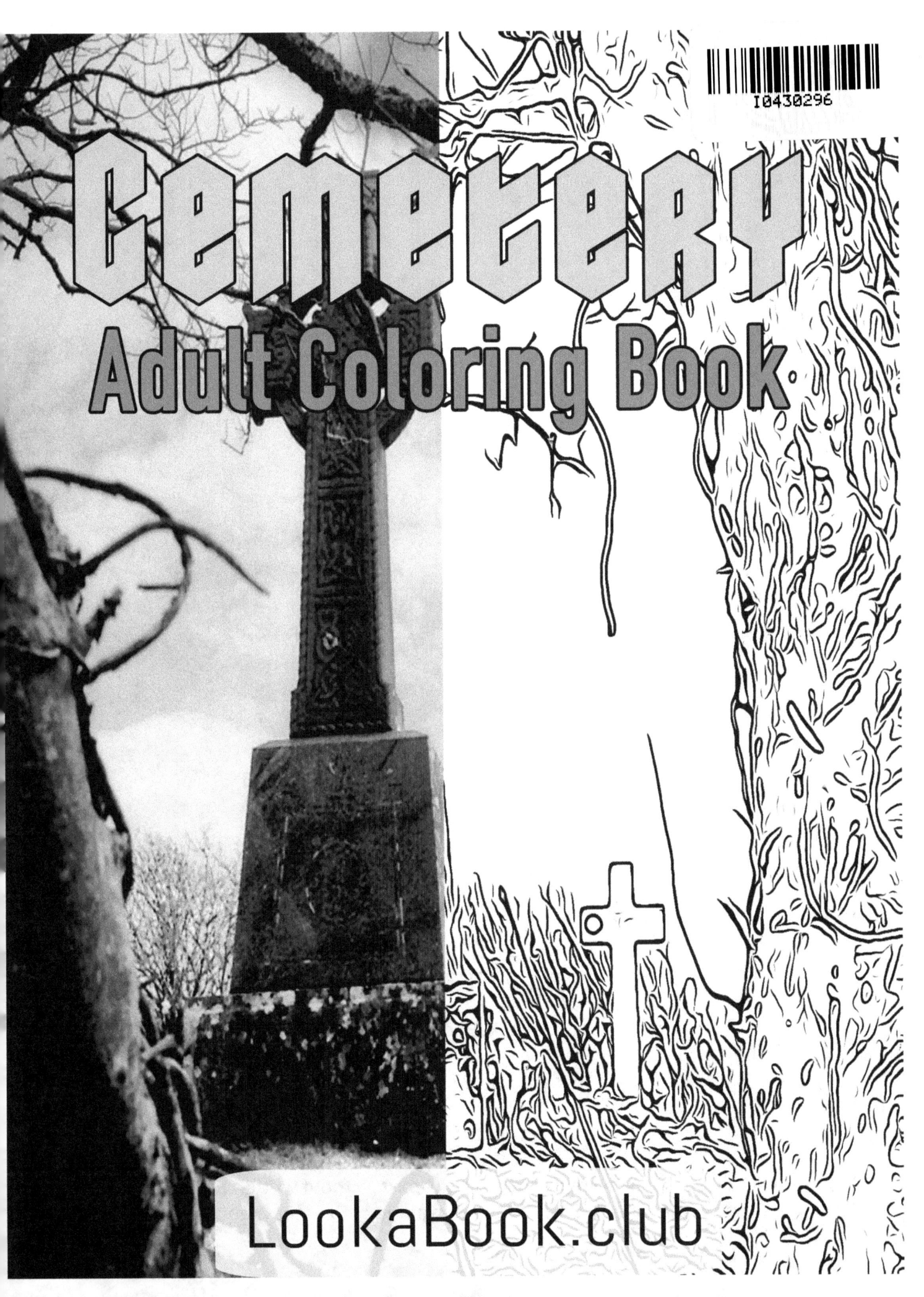

ISBN: 9798372304550

LookaBook.club

Copyright © 2023 by Dale Curwin

All rights reserved.

No portion of this book may be reproduced in any form without written permission from the publisher or author, except as permitted by U.S. copyright law.

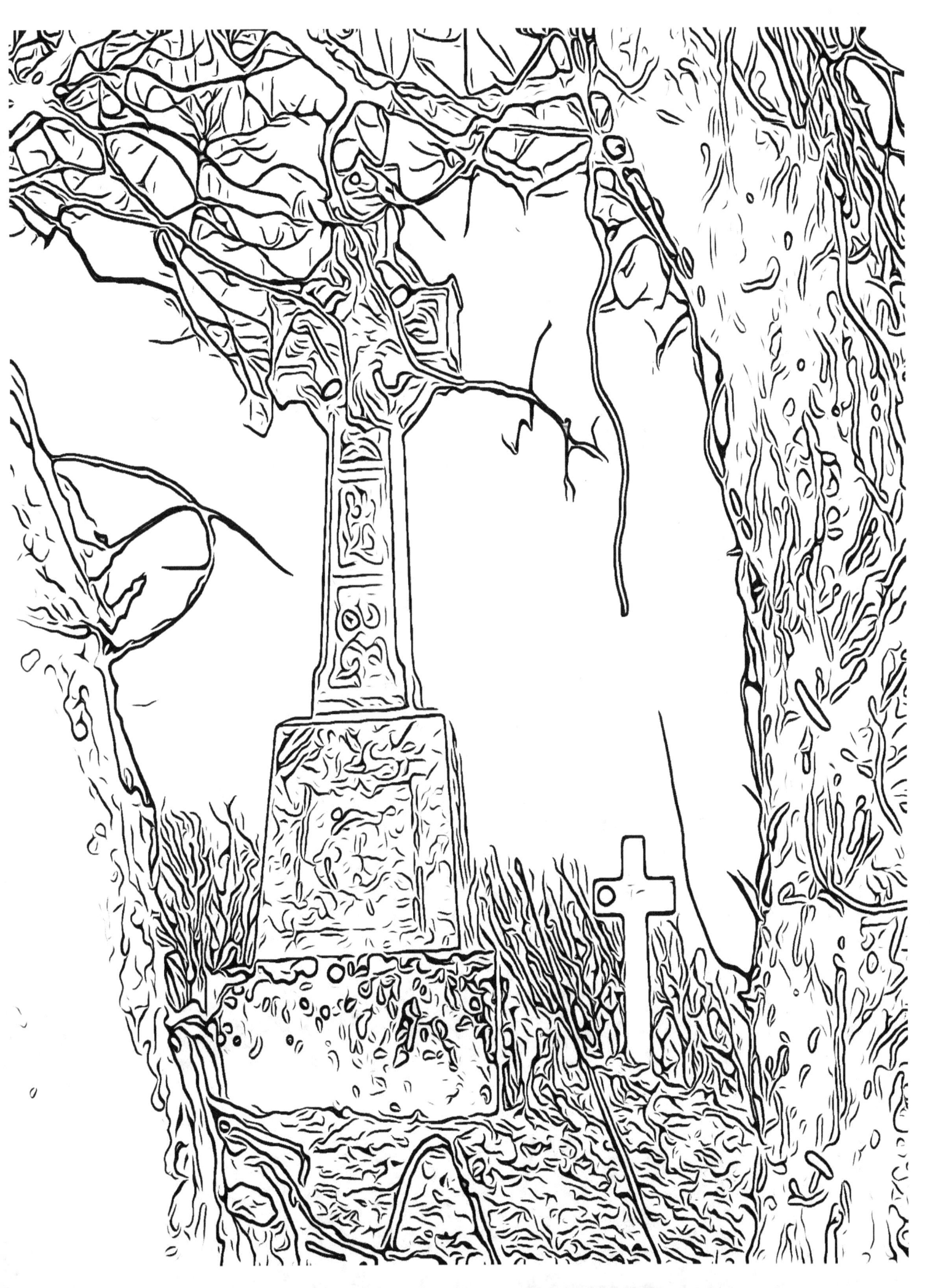

> Our dead are never
> dead to us
> until we have
> forgotten them
> – George Eliot

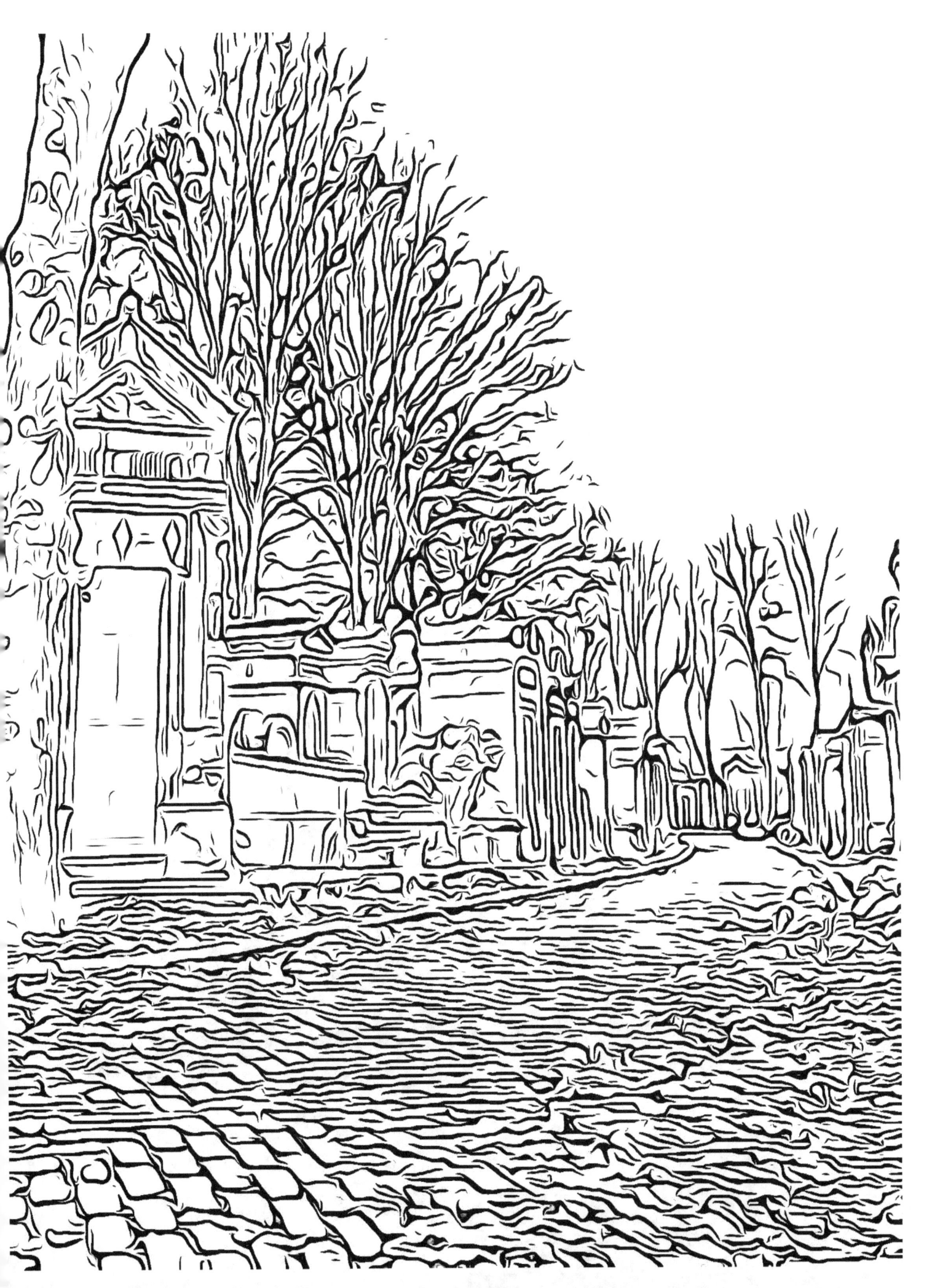

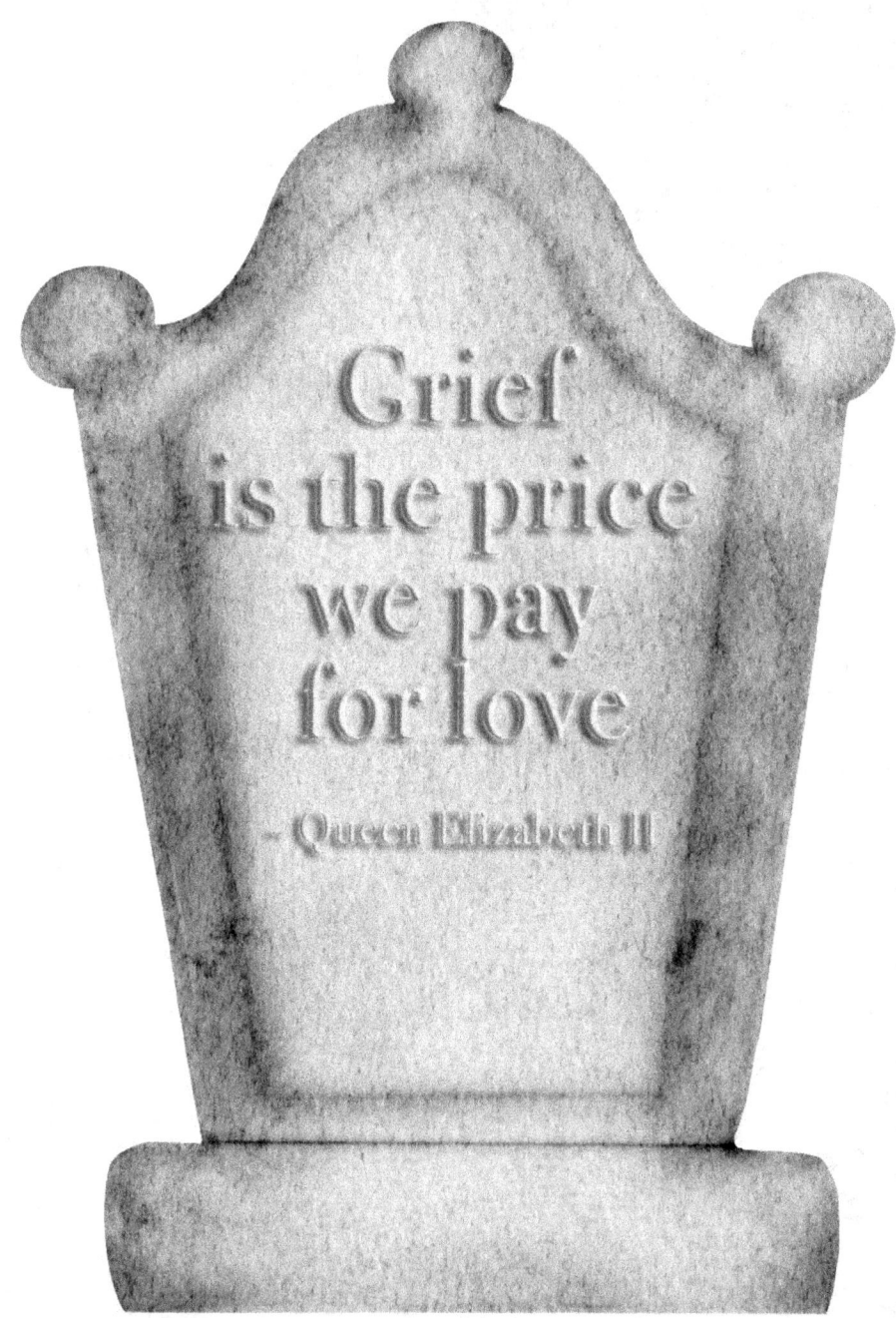

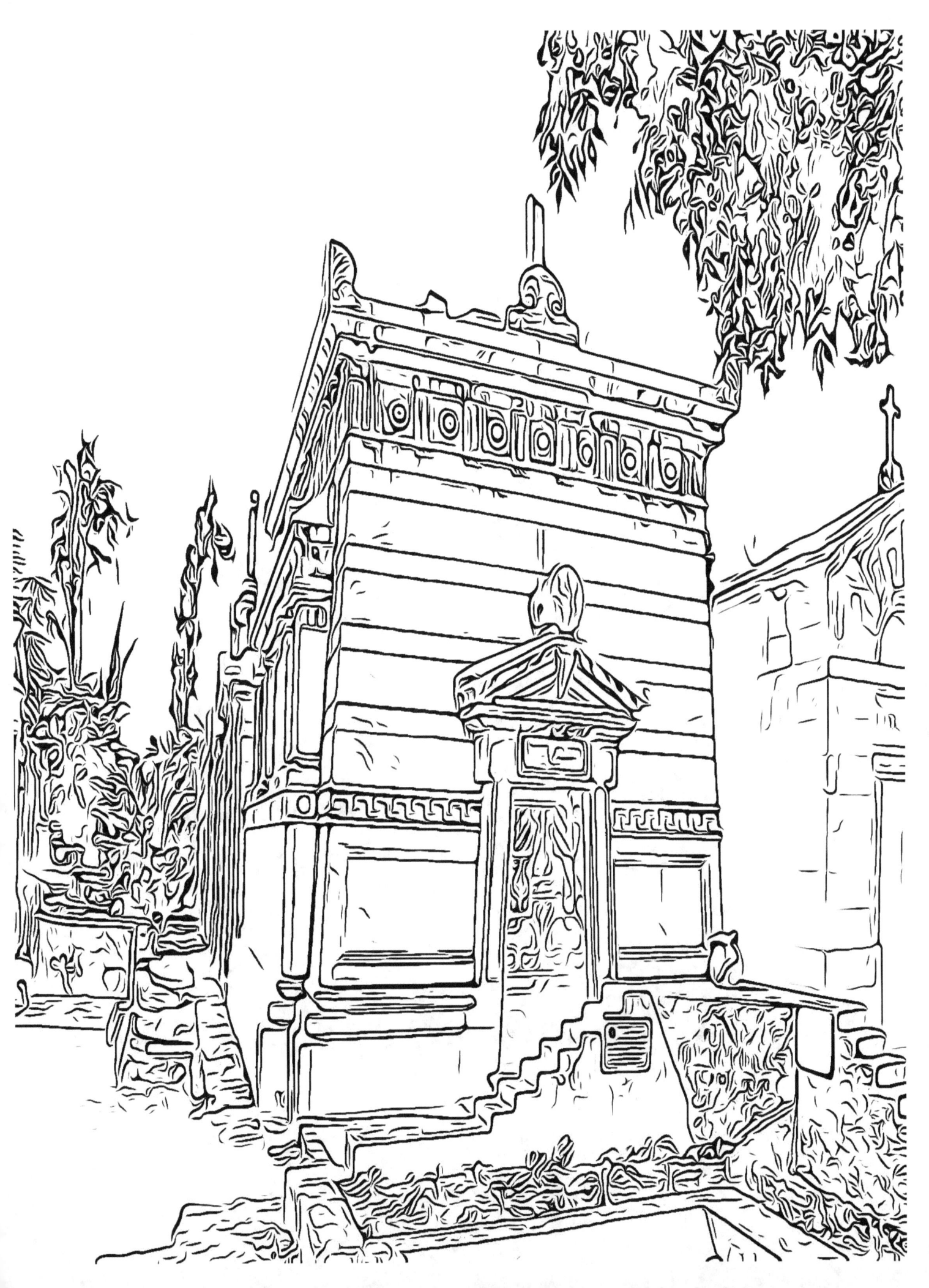

> At my age I do
> what Mark Twain did
> I get my daily paper
> look at the obituaries
> page and if I'm not there
> I carry on as usual
> – Patrick Moore

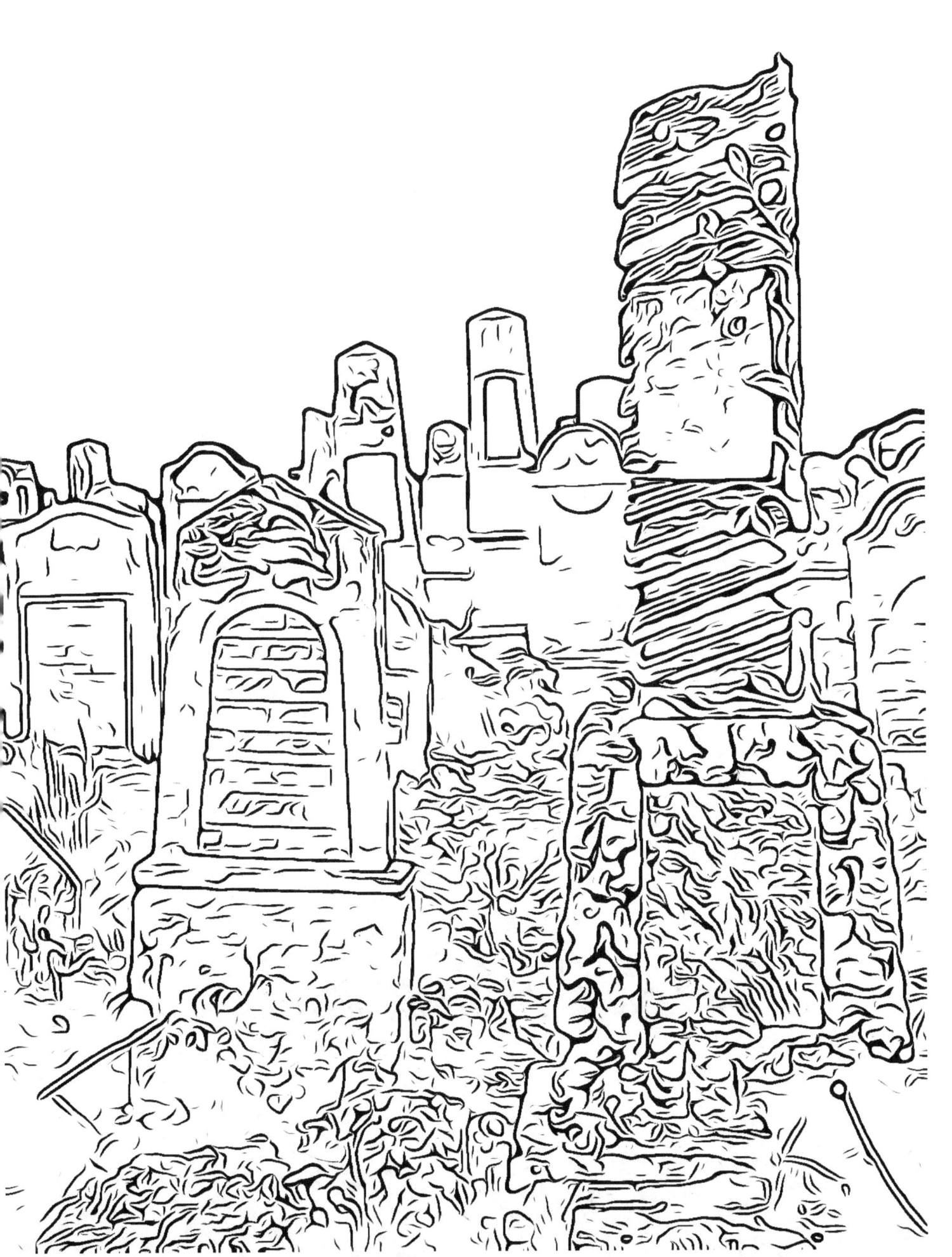

> Our death is not an end
> if we can live on in our
> children and the younger
> generation
> For they are us;
> our bodies are only
> wilted leaves on
> the tree of life
> — Albert Einstein

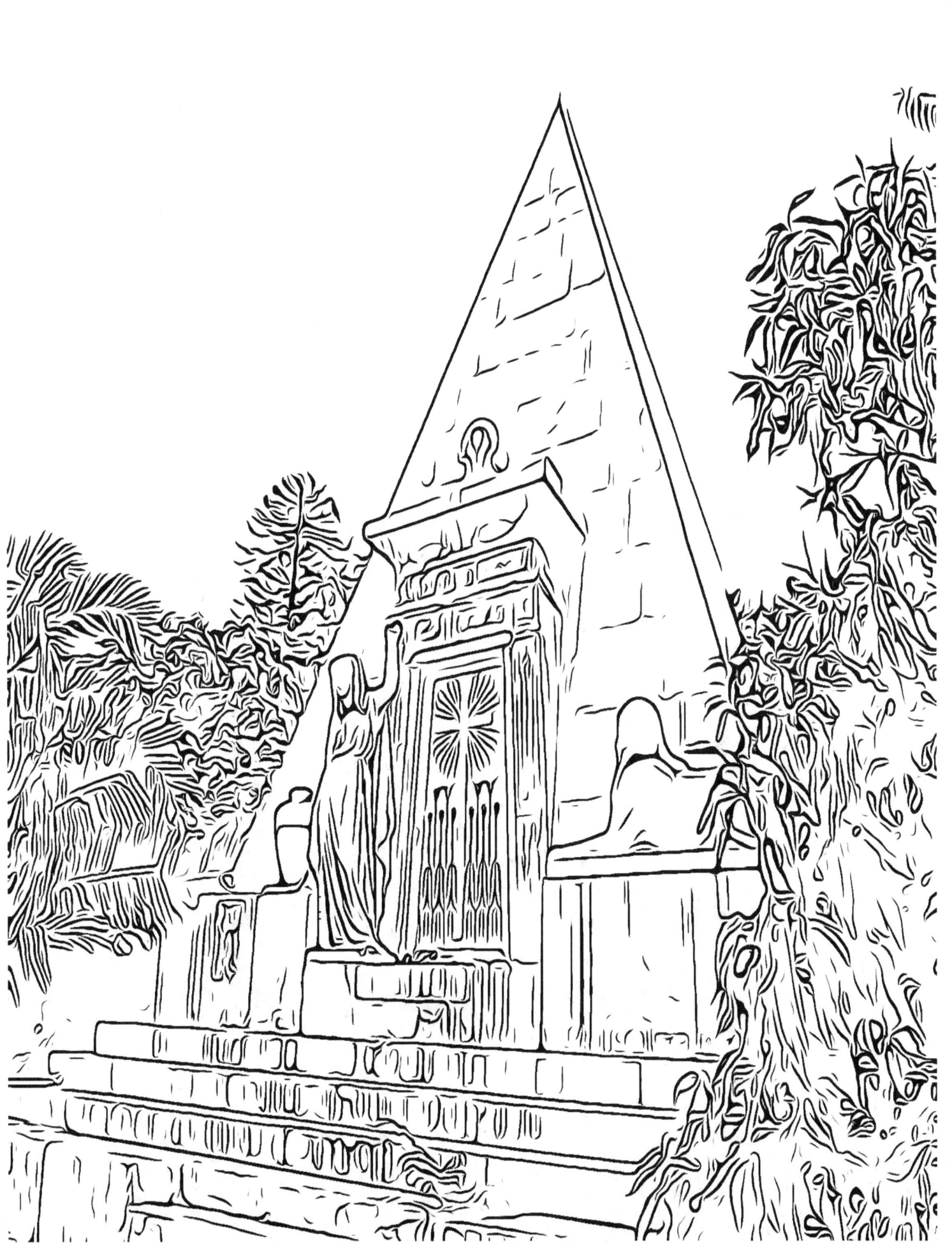

> After all what's
> a life anyway?
> We're born
> we live
> a little while
> we die
> — E.B. White

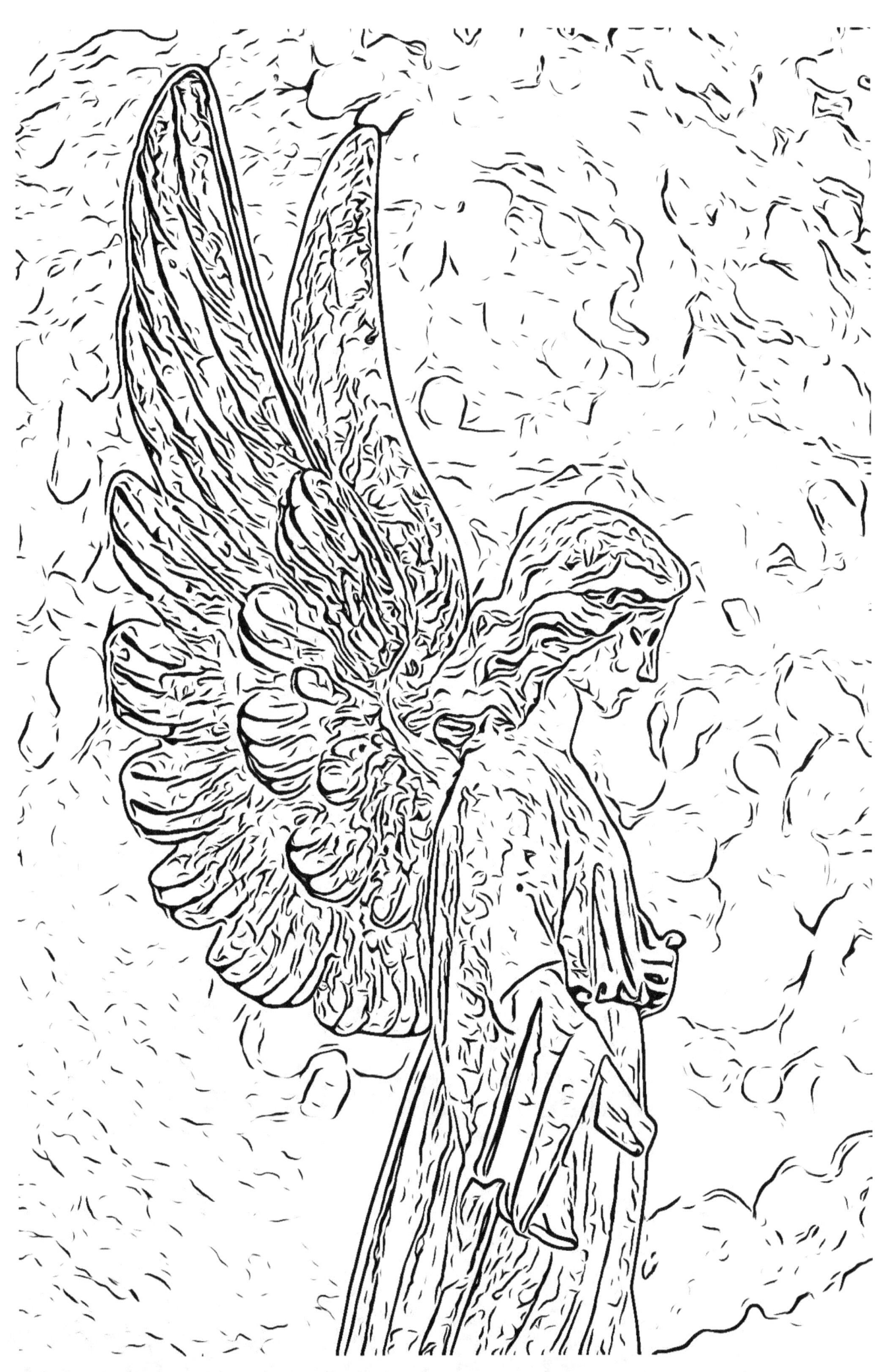

Death is no more
than passing from
one room into
another
But there's a
difference for me
you know
Because in that
other room
I shall be able to see
— Helen Keller

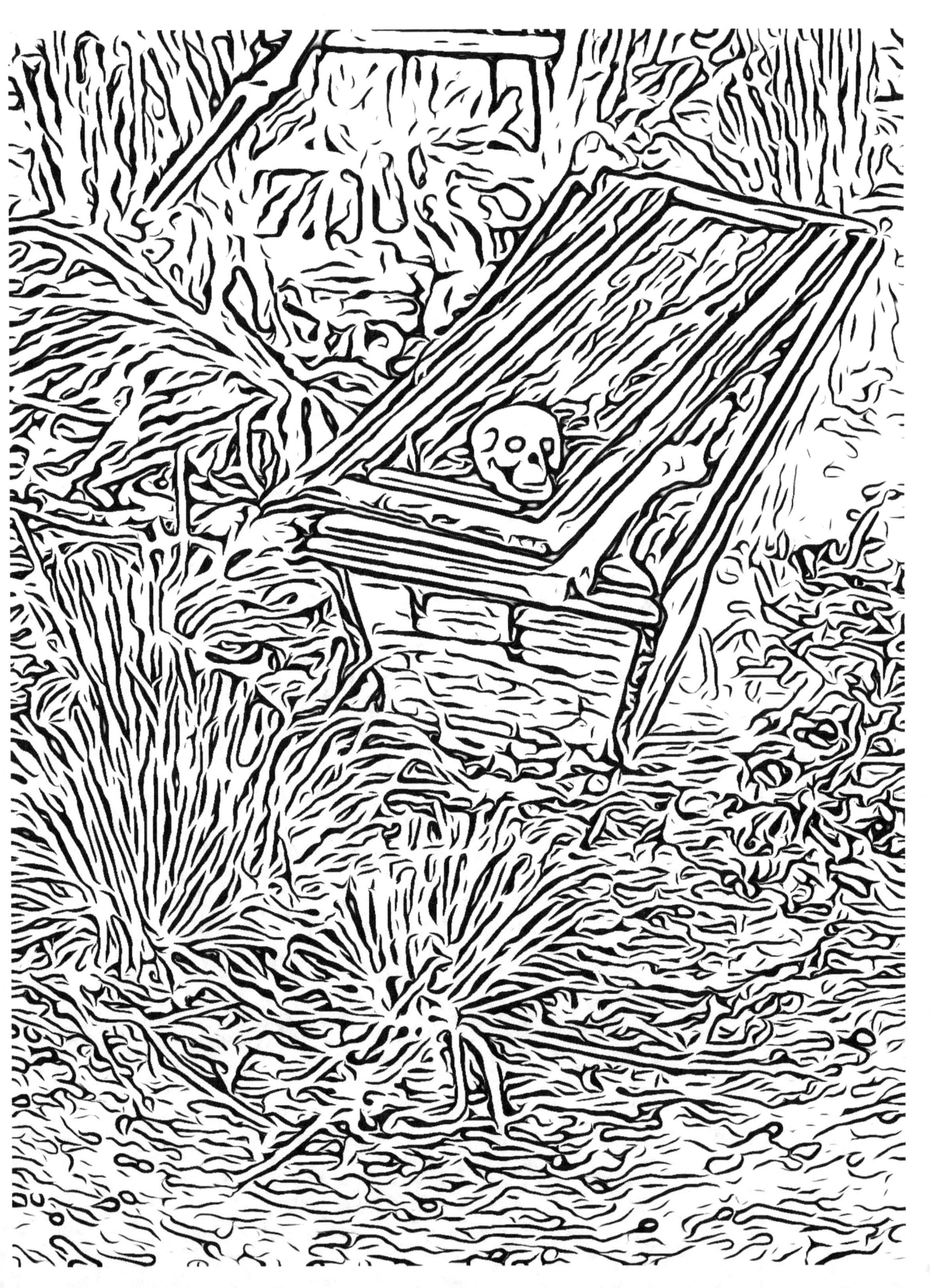

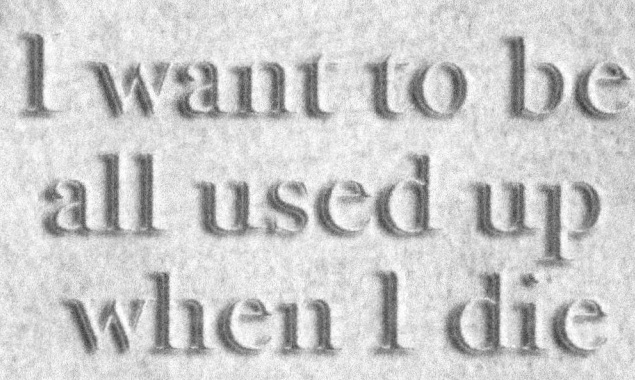

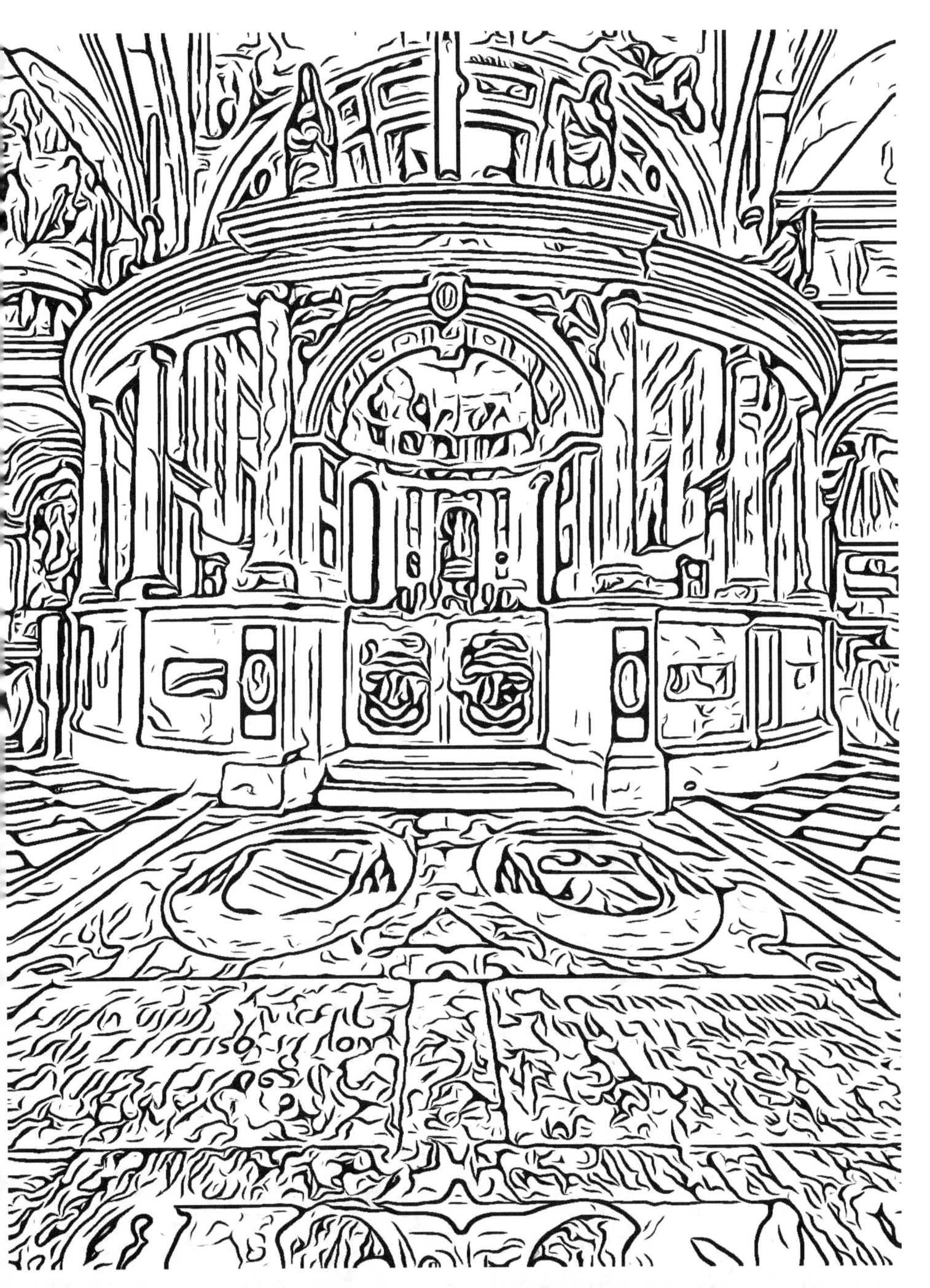

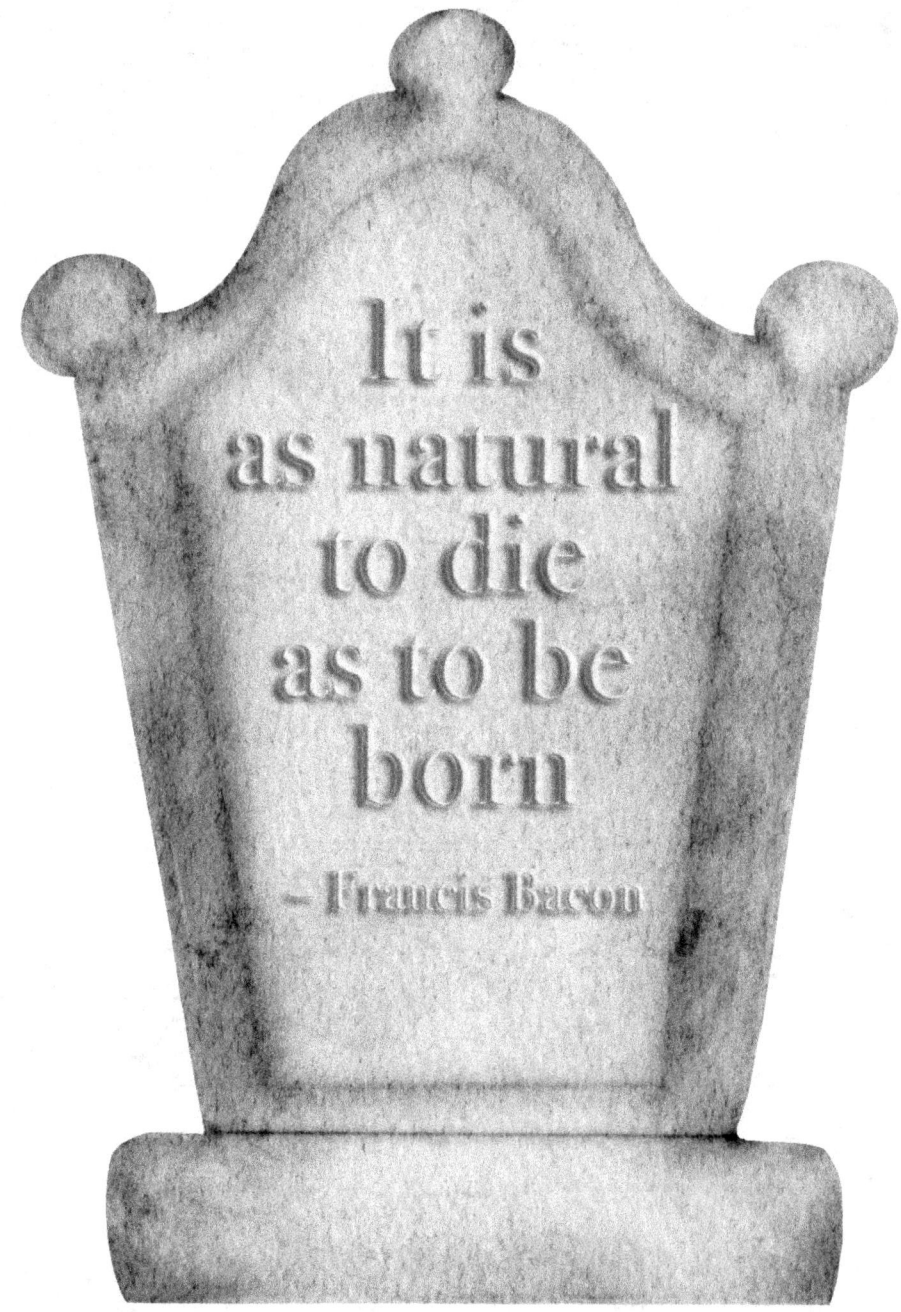

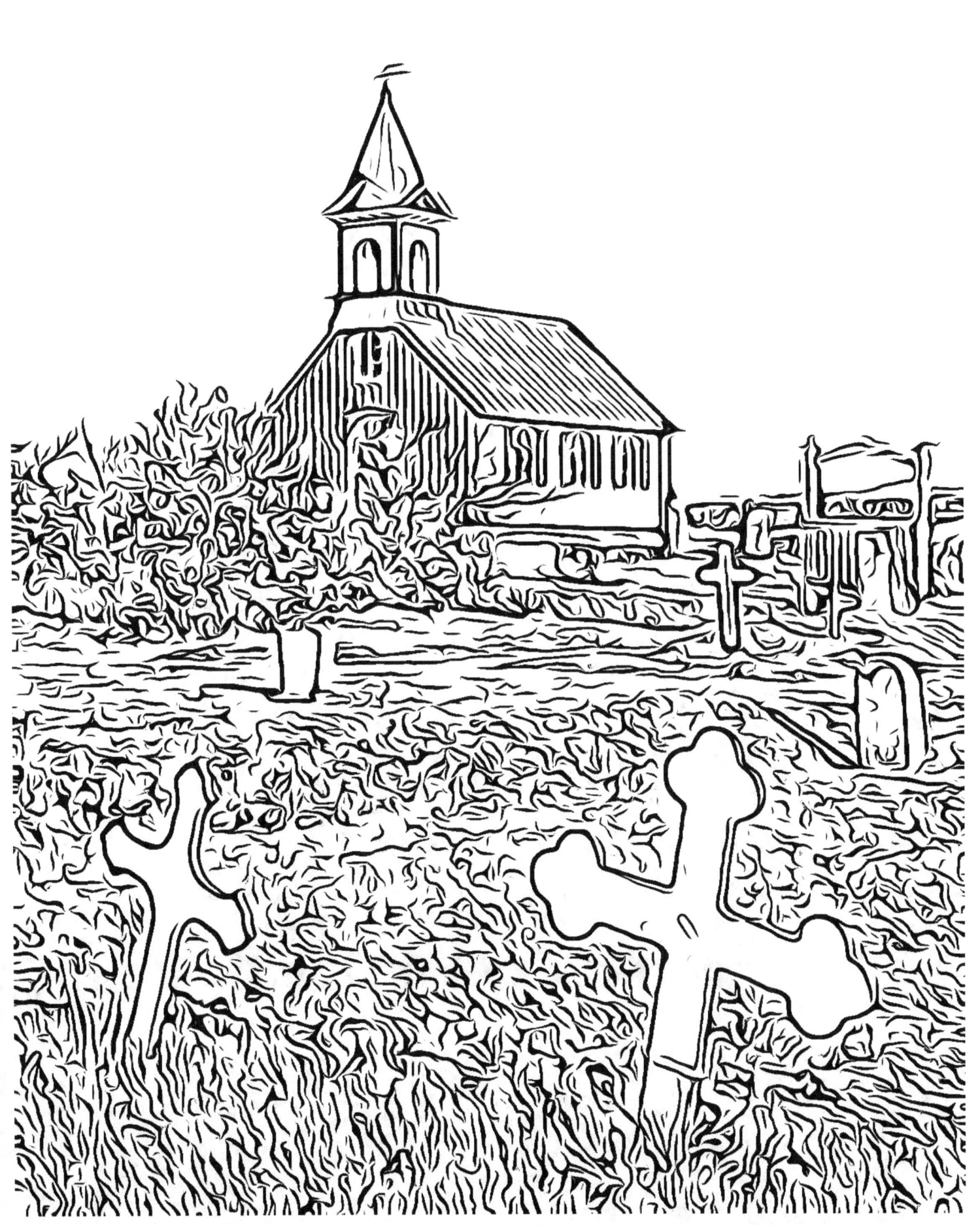

> When you've told someone that you've left them a legacy the only decent thing to do is to die at once
> – Samuel Butler

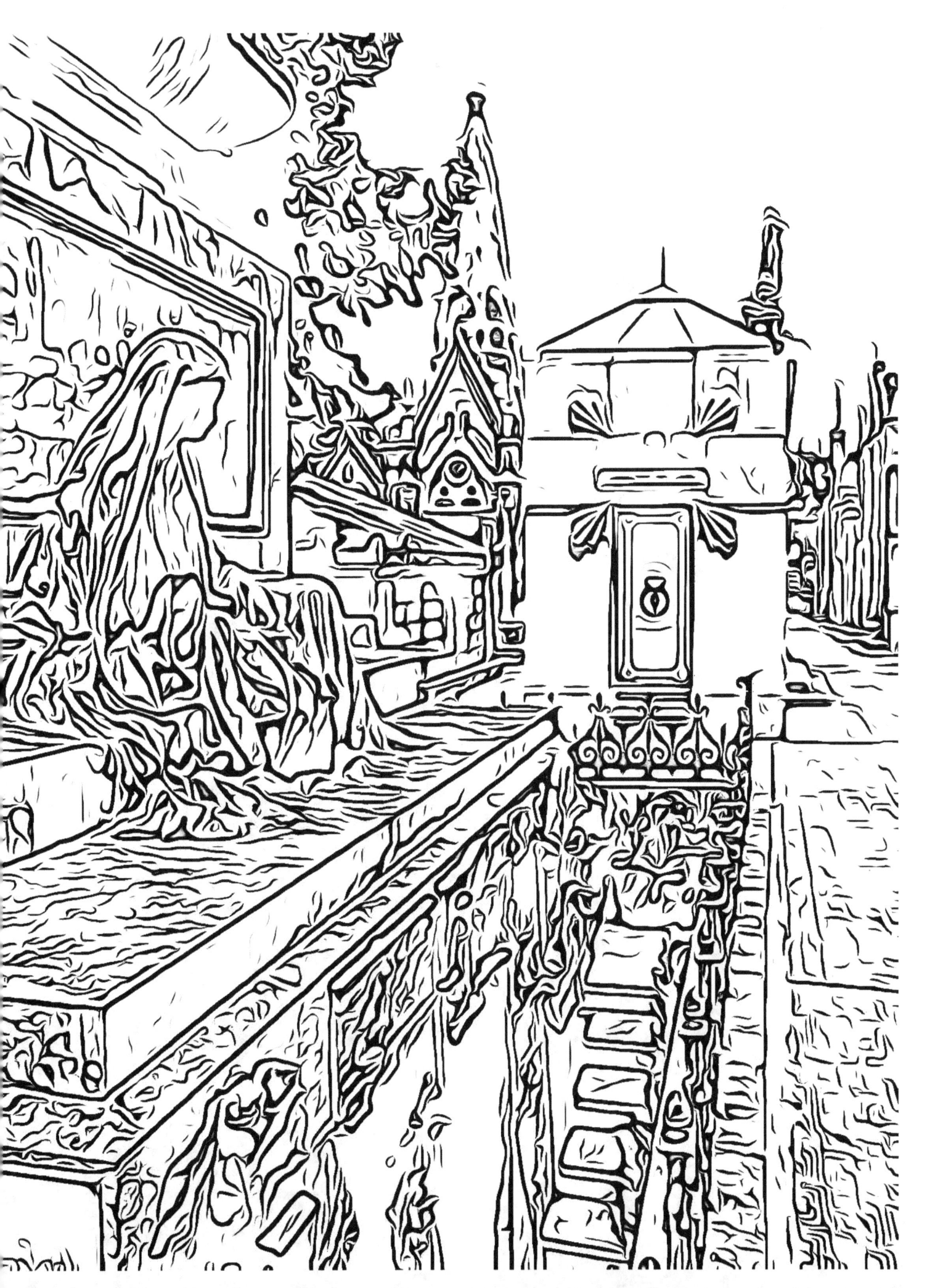

> It matters not
> how a man dies
> but how he lives
> The act of dying is not
> of importance
> it lasts so short a time
>
> – Samuel Johnson

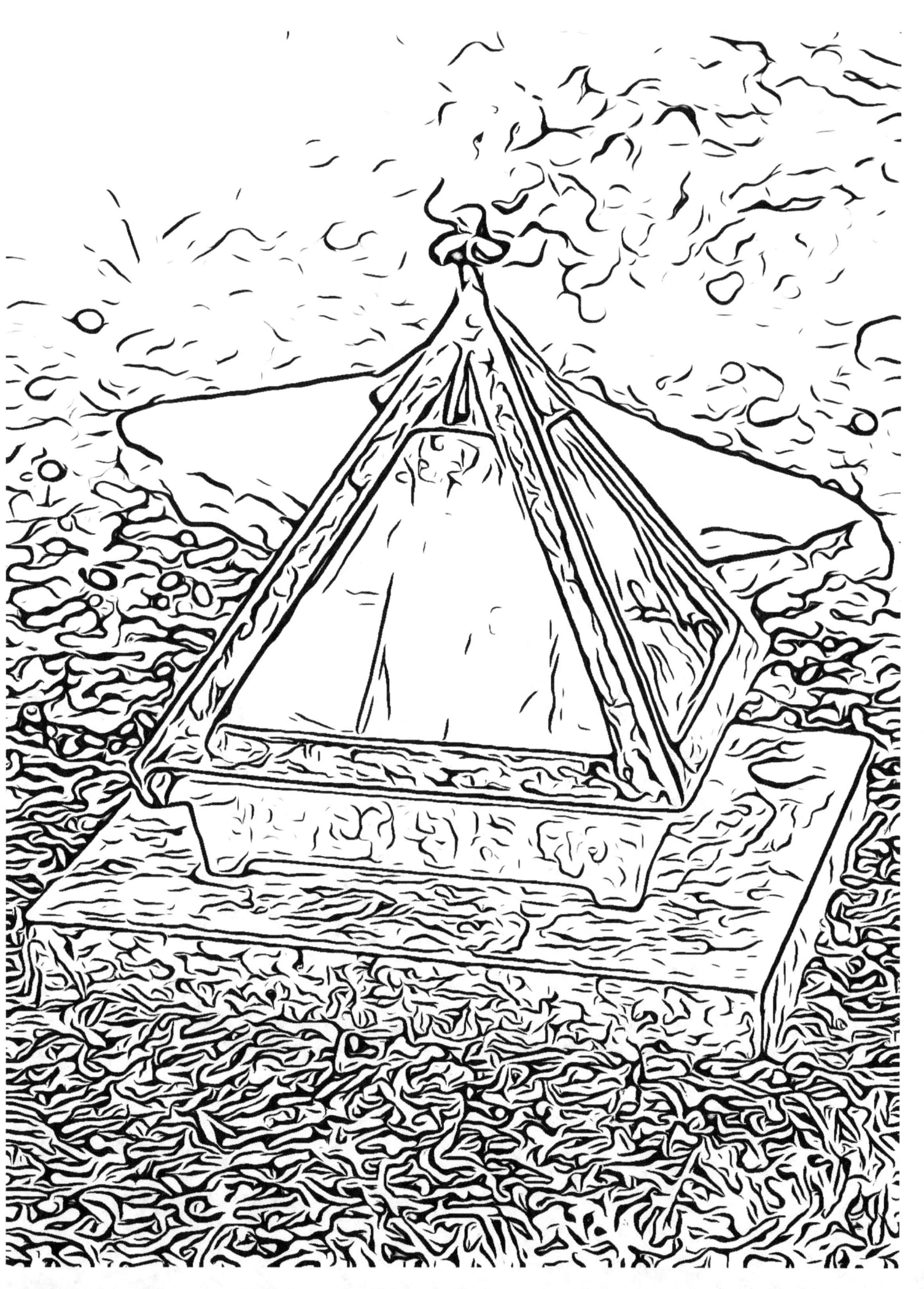

> We all die
> The goal isn't
> to live forever
> the goal is to
> create something
> that will
> — Chuck Palahniuk

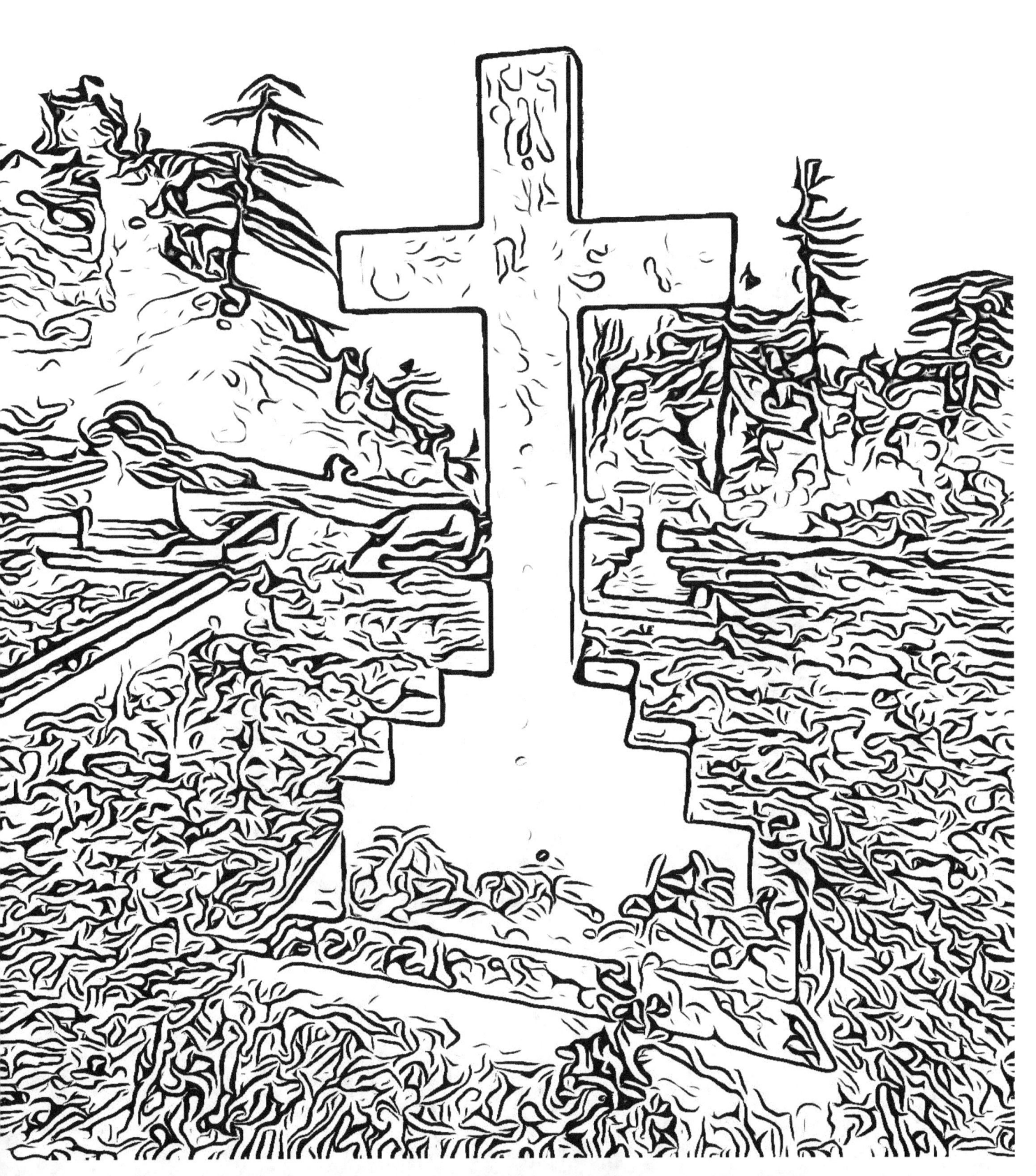

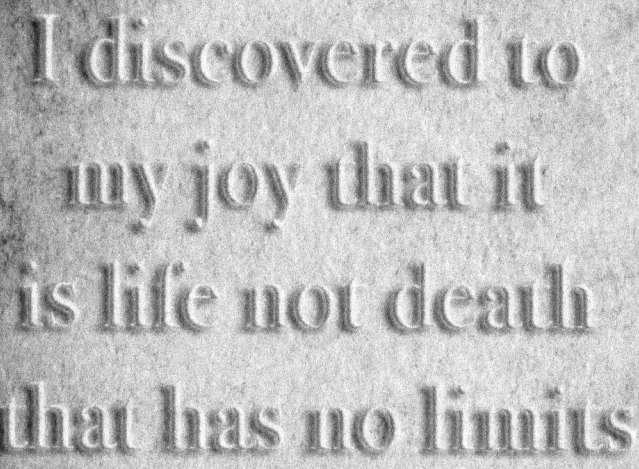

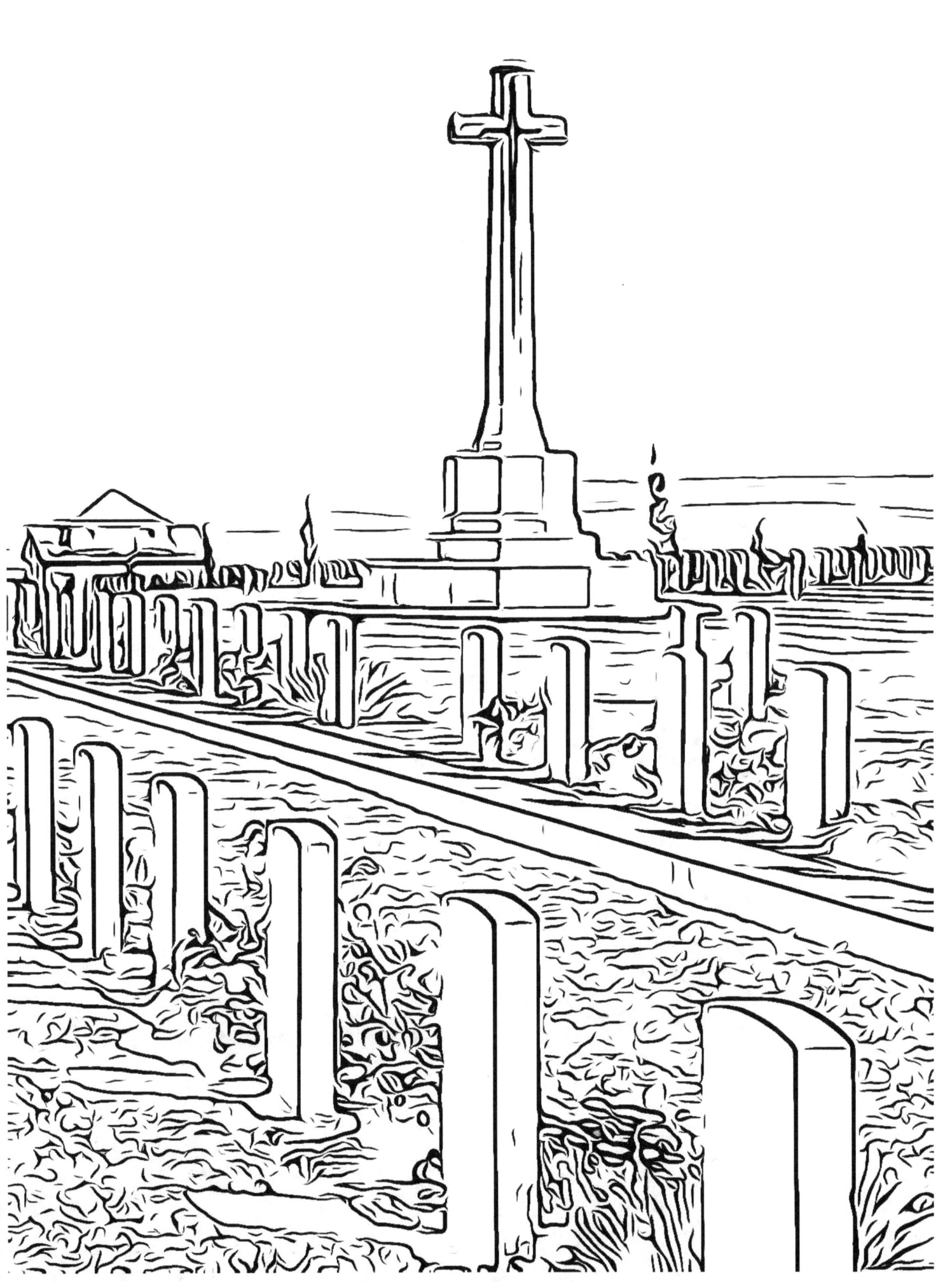

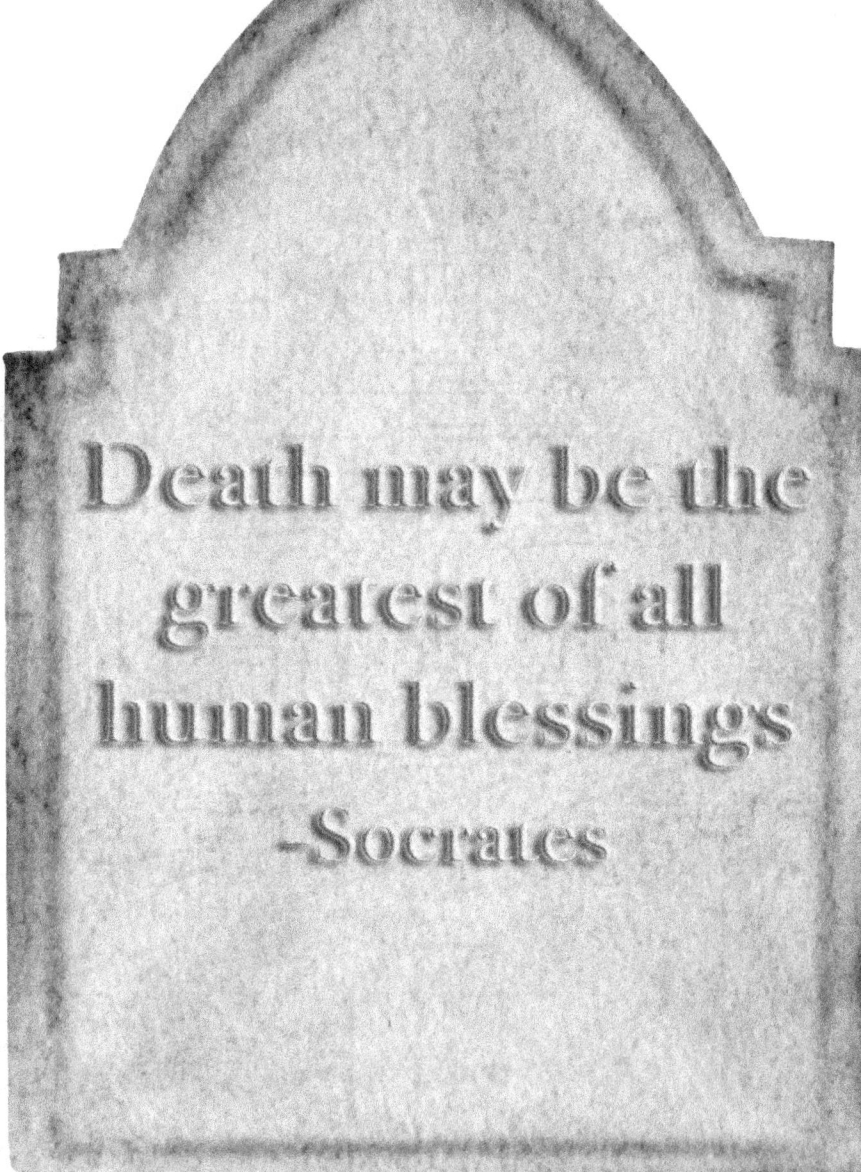

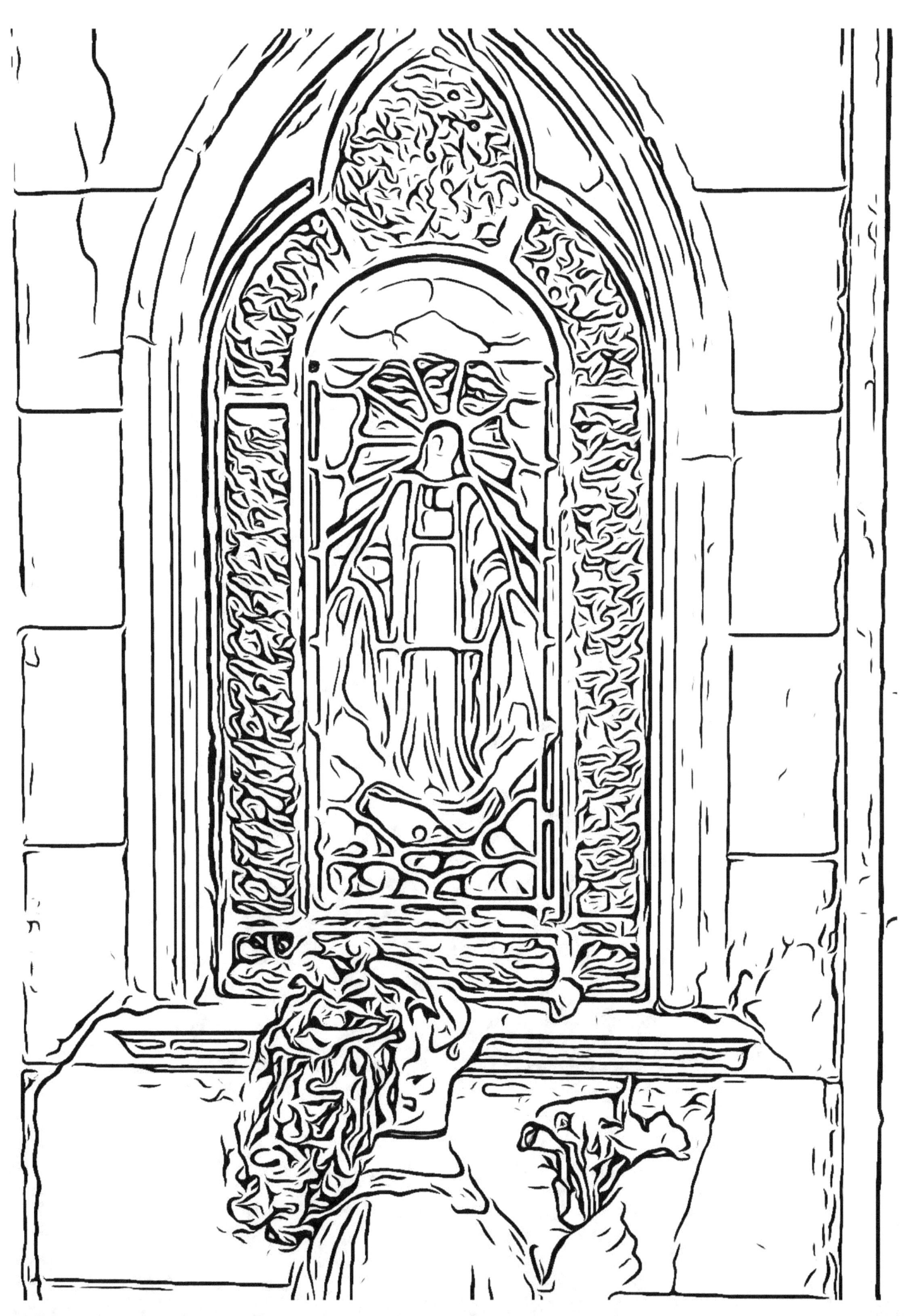

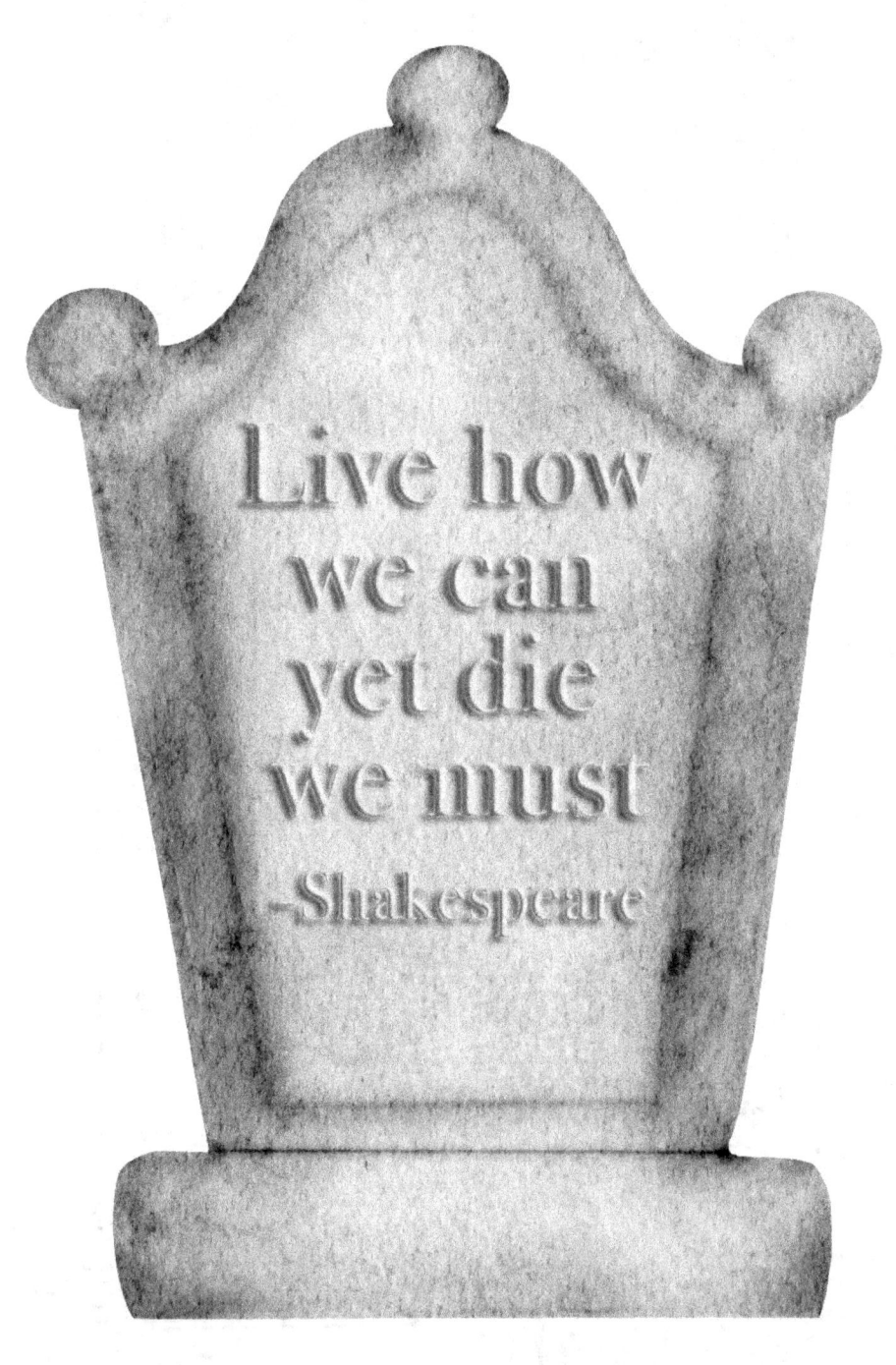

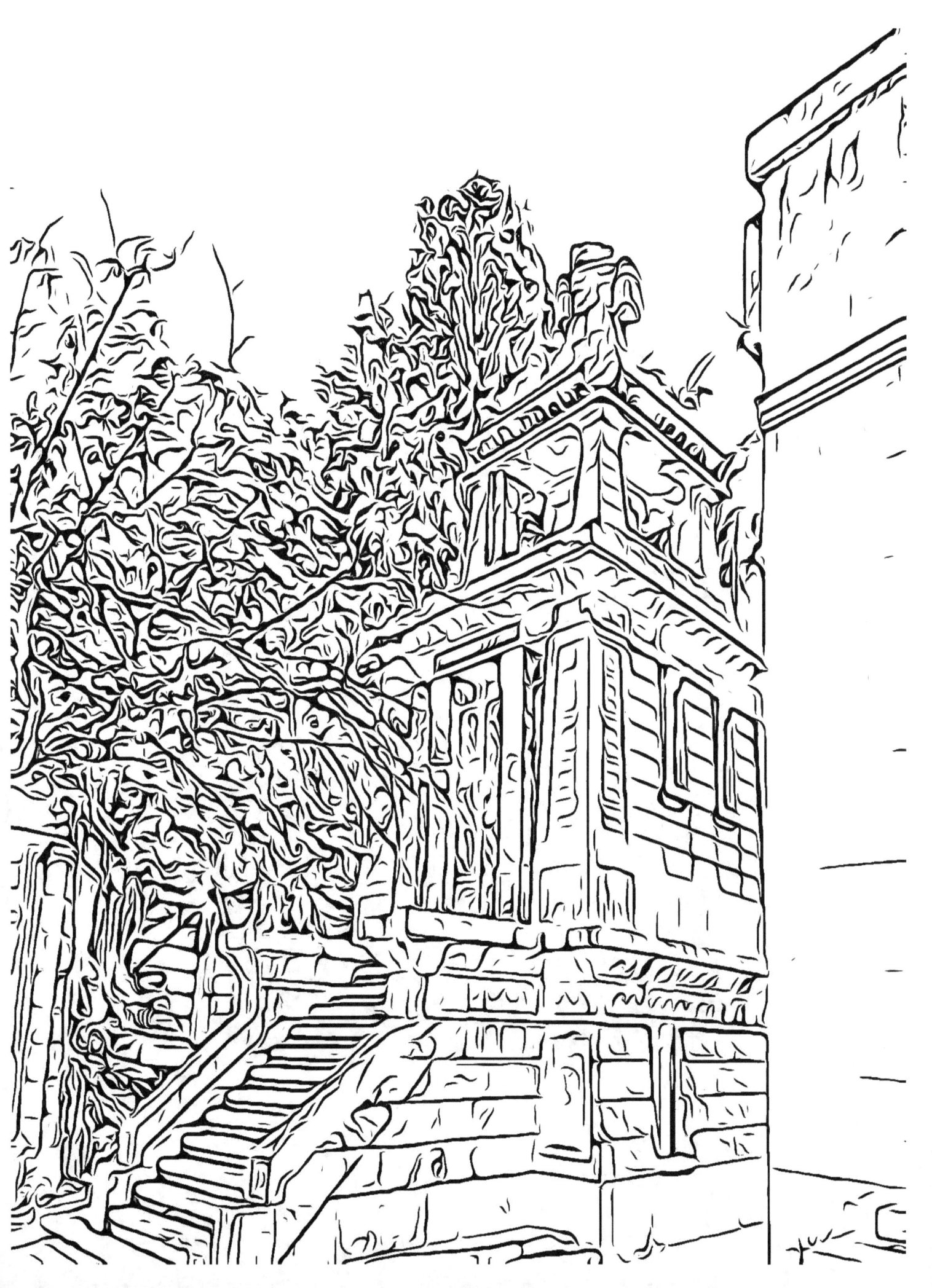

> I am ready to meet my maker, but whether my maker is prepared for the great ordeal of meeting me is another matter
>
> – Winston Churchill

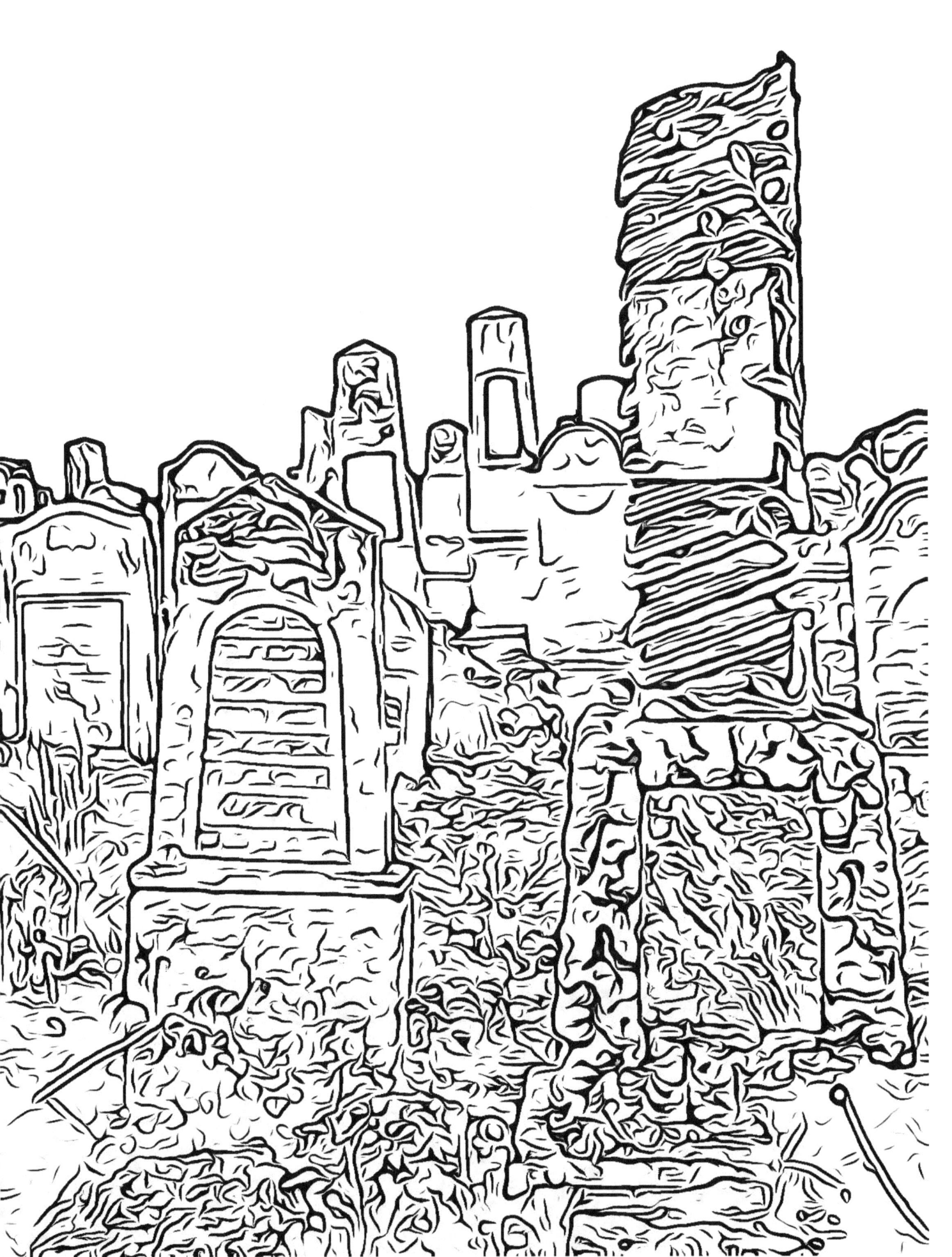

> Man alone chimes
> the hour and because
> of this man alone suffers
> a paralyzing fear that
> no other creature endures
> A fear of time running out
>
> – Mitch Albom

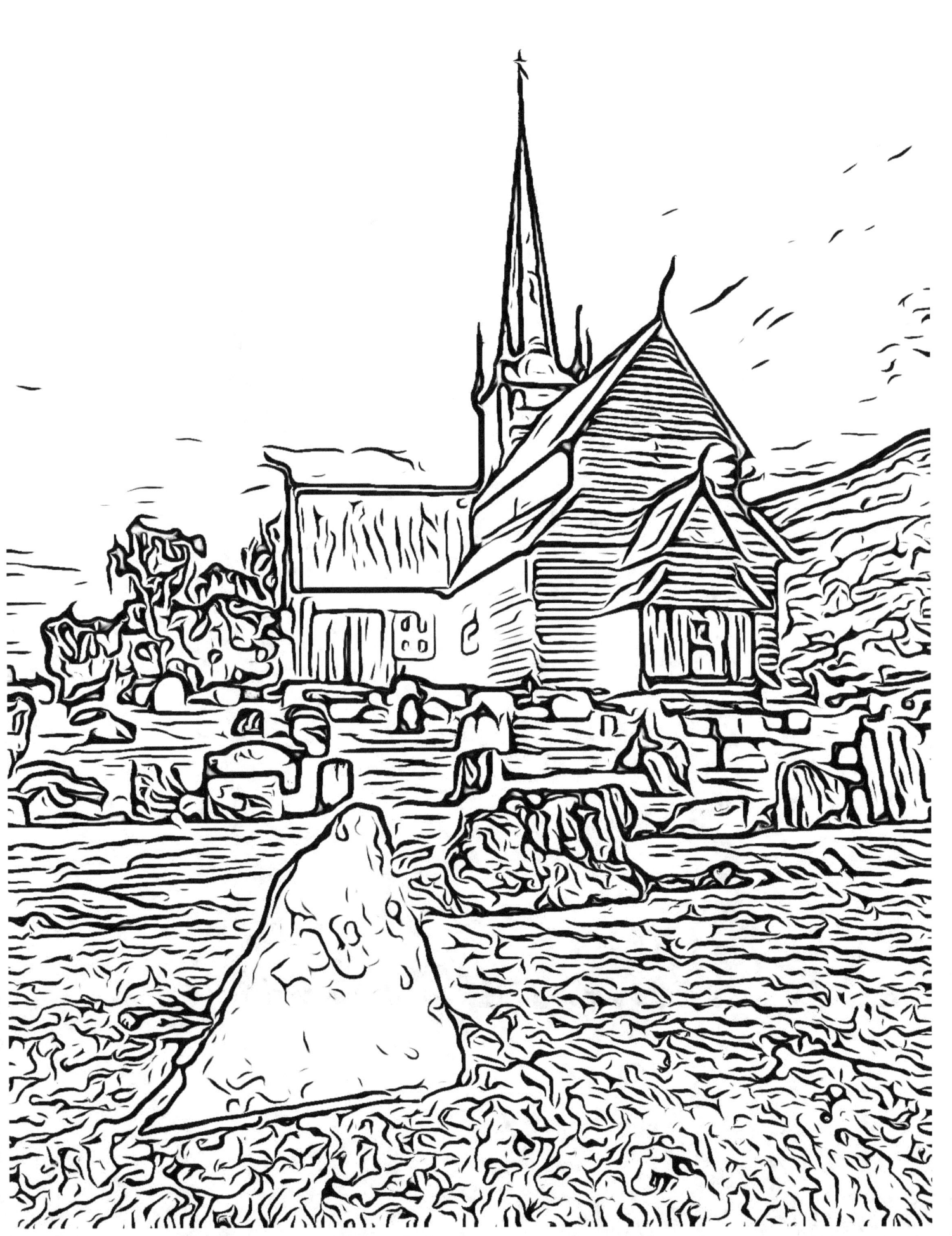

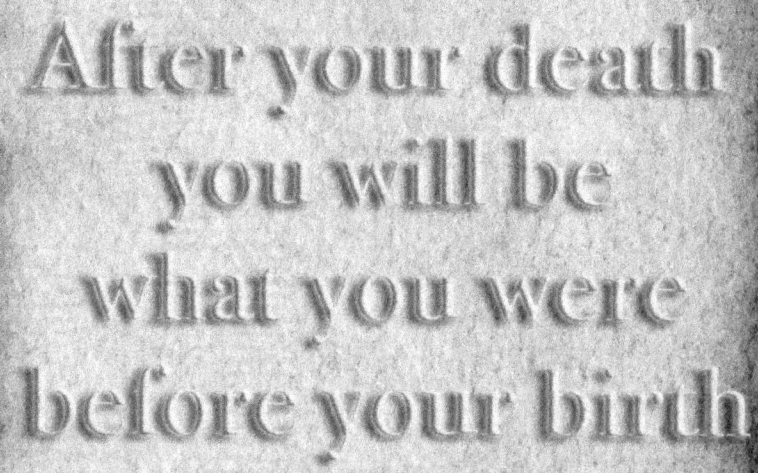

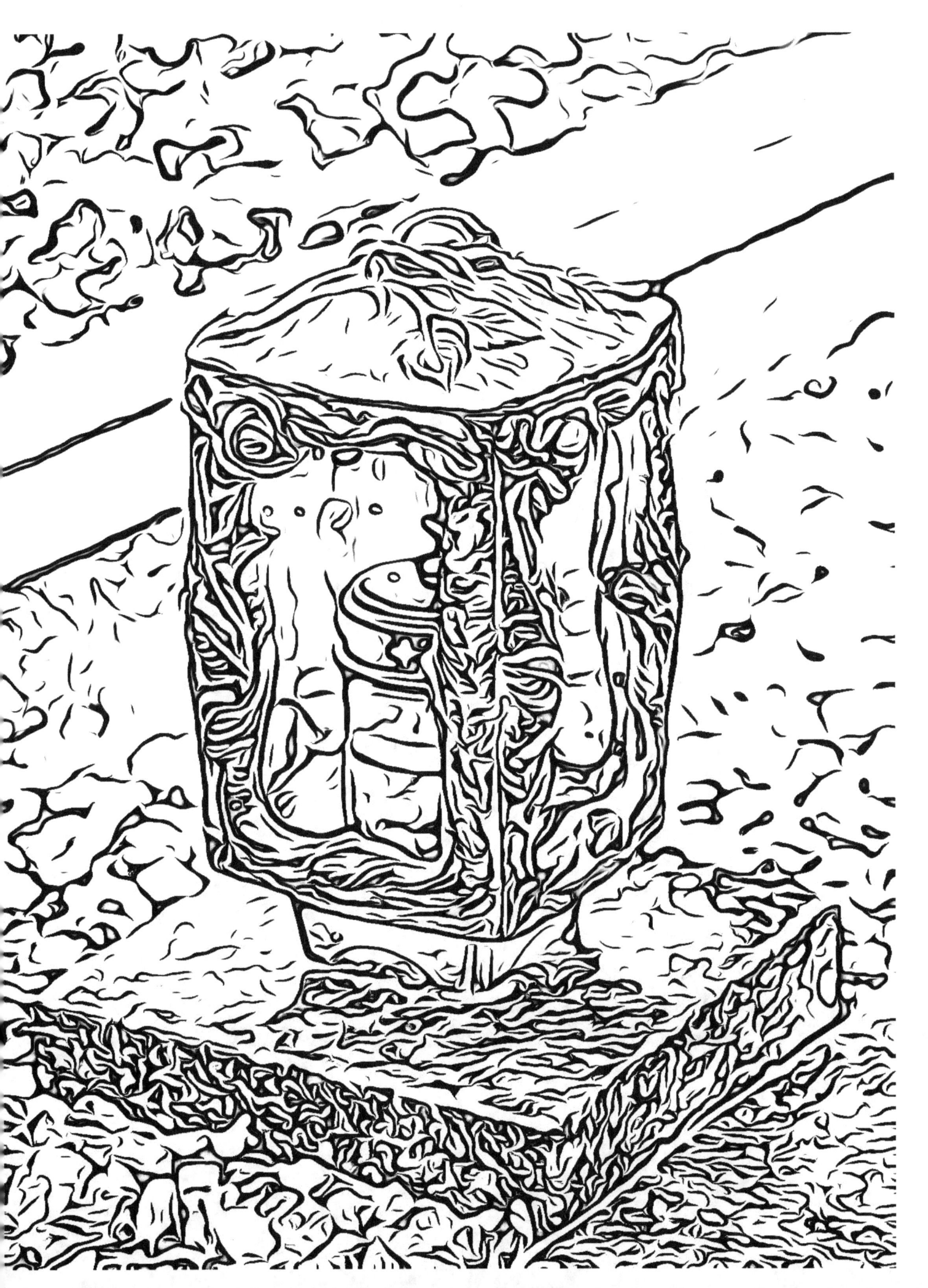

Death must be
so beautiful
To lie in the soft
brown earth with
the grasses waving
above one's head
and listen to silence
— Oscar Wilde

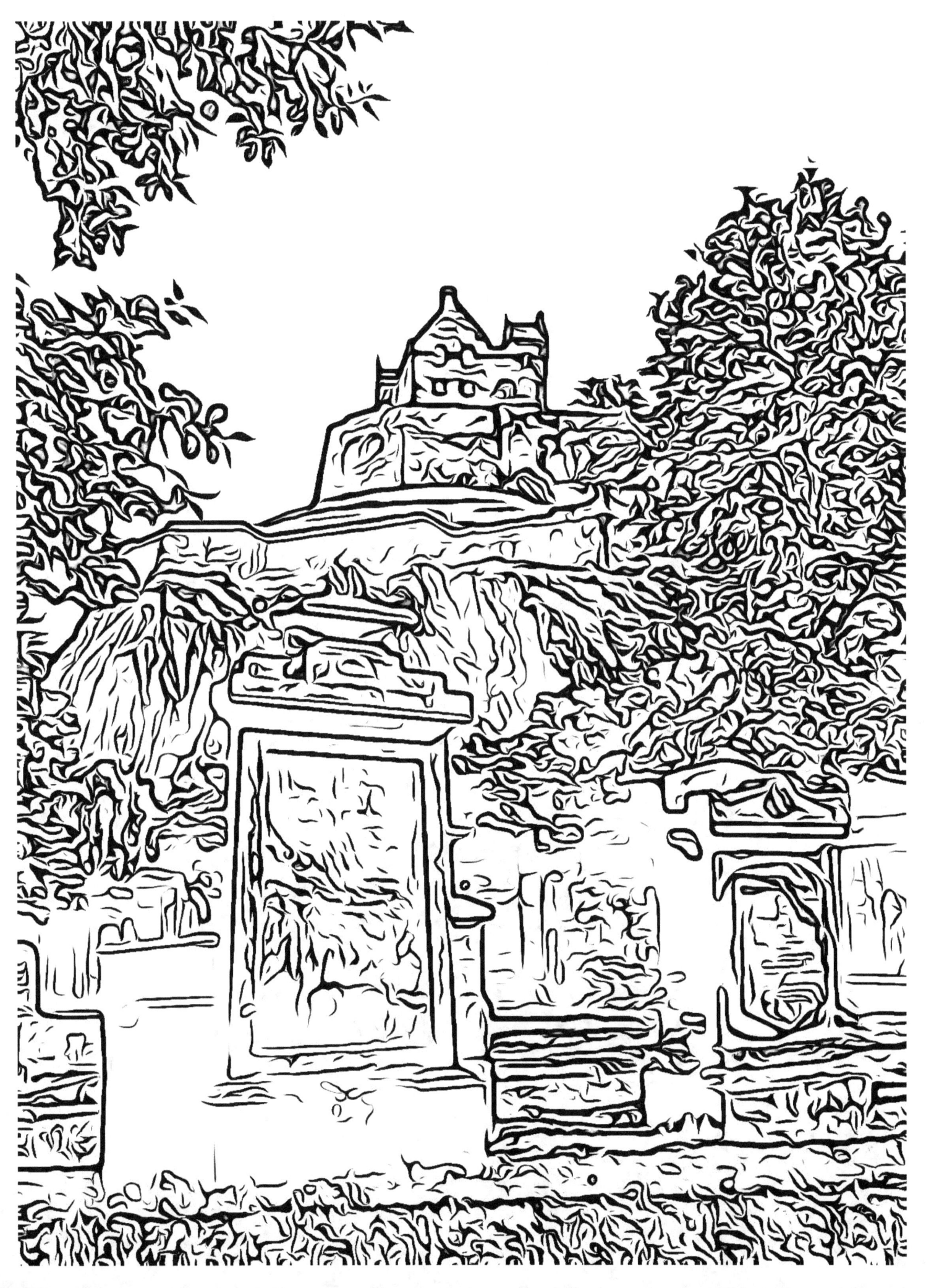

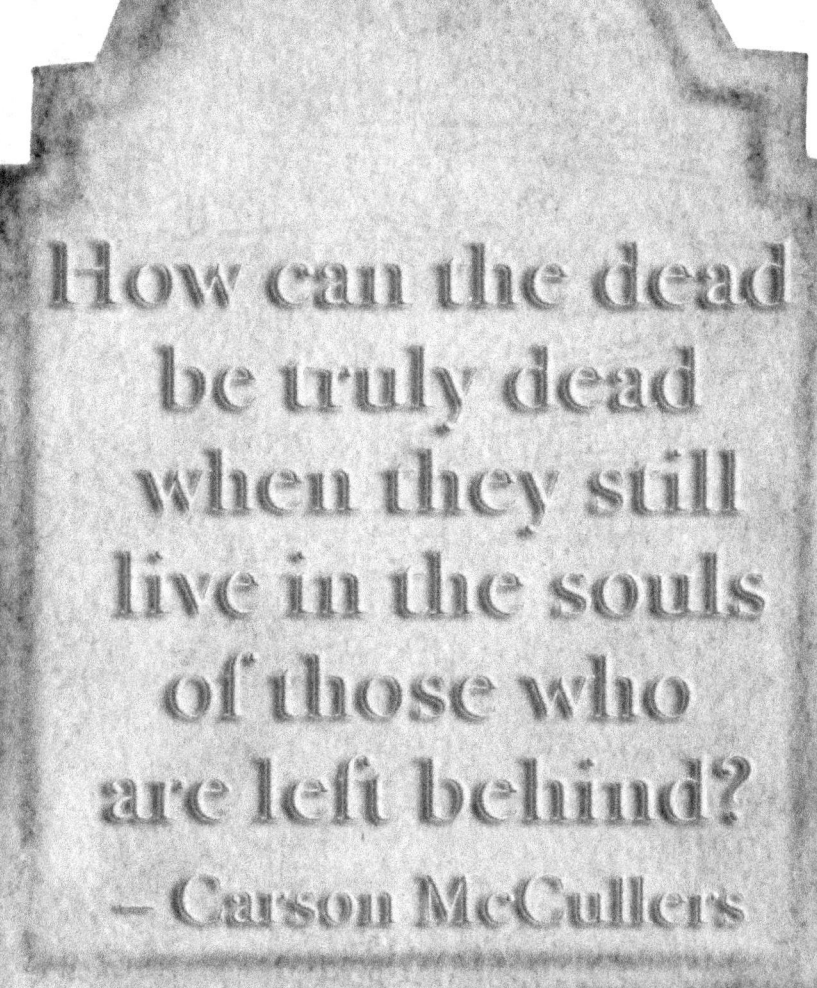

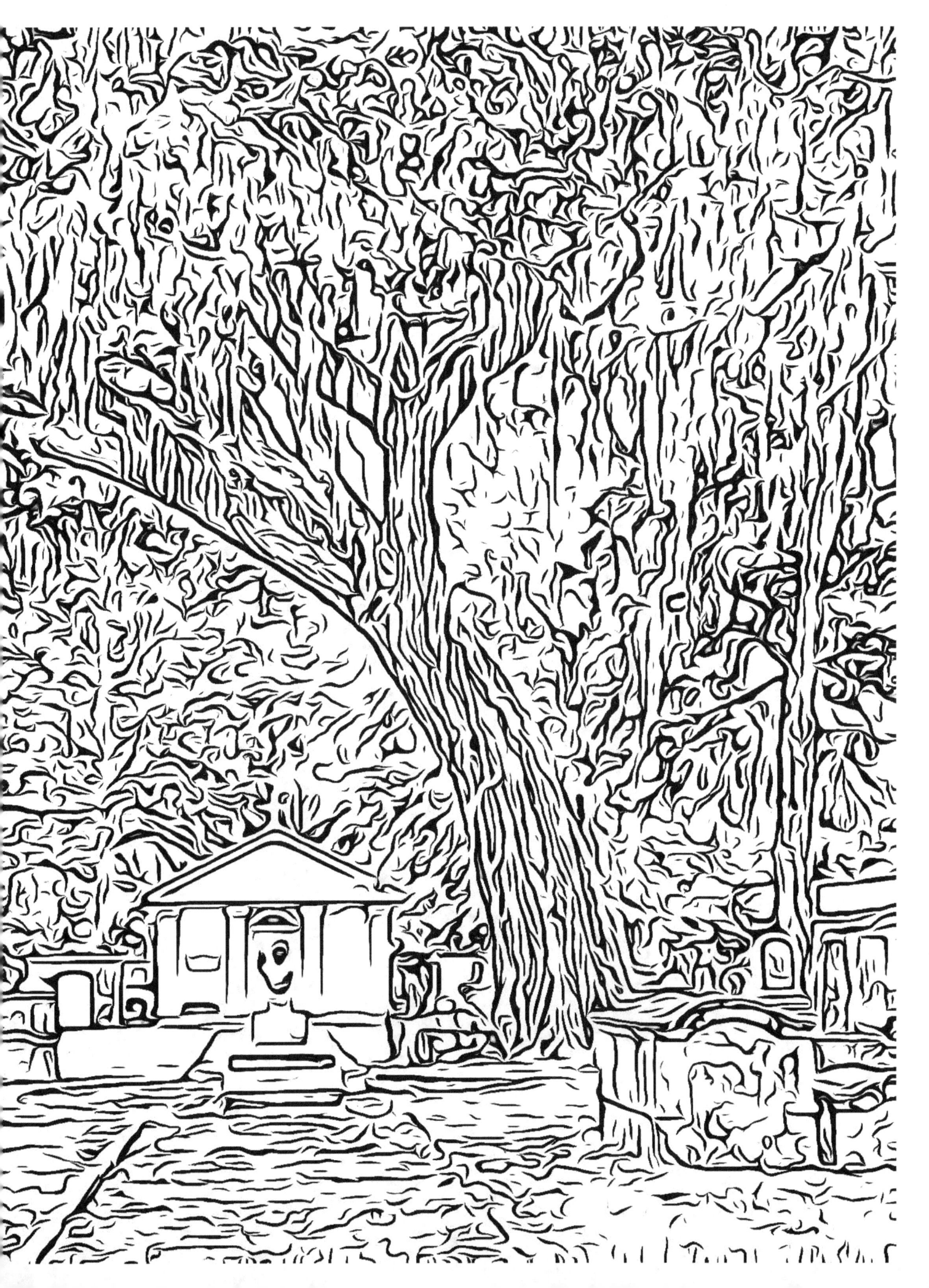

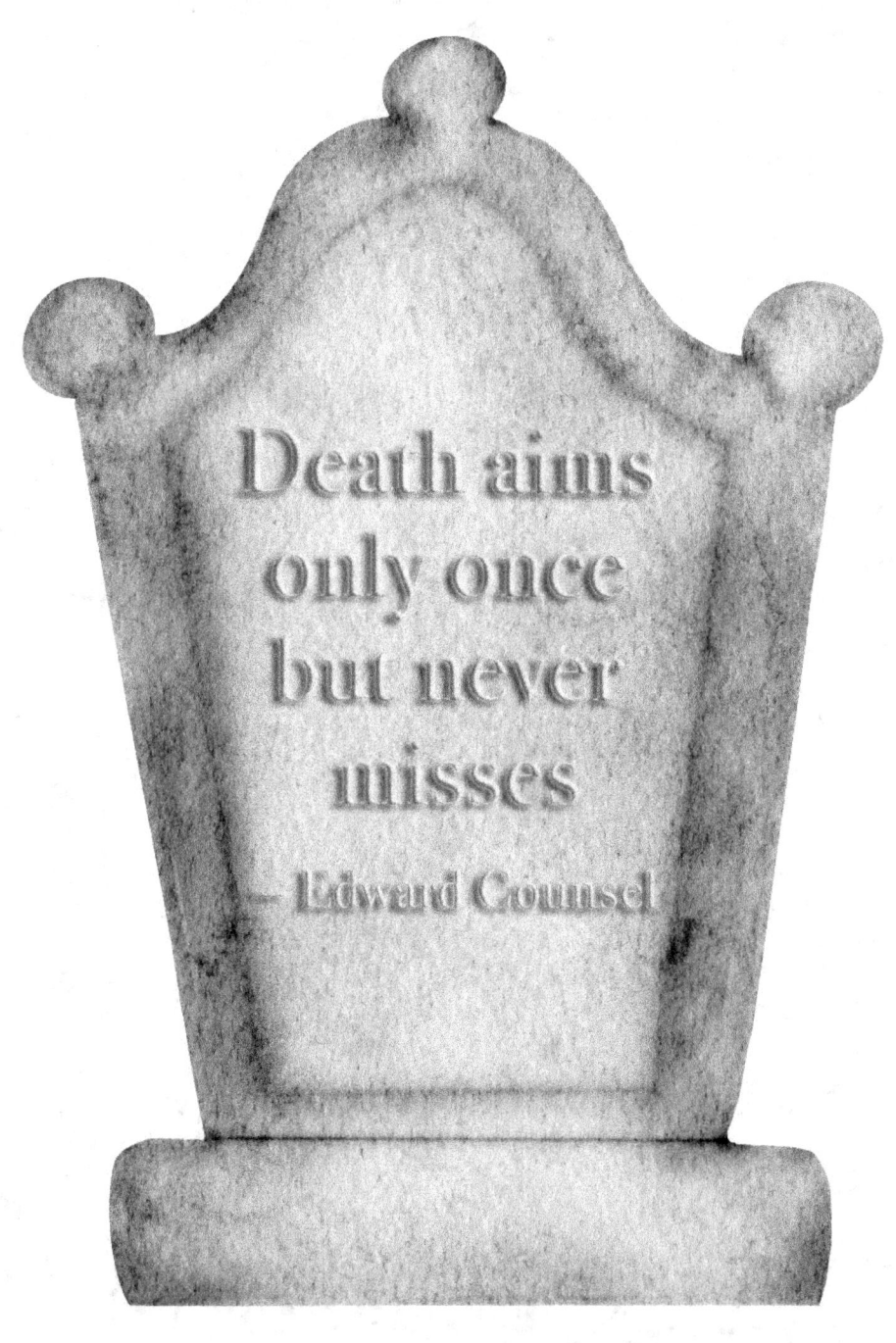

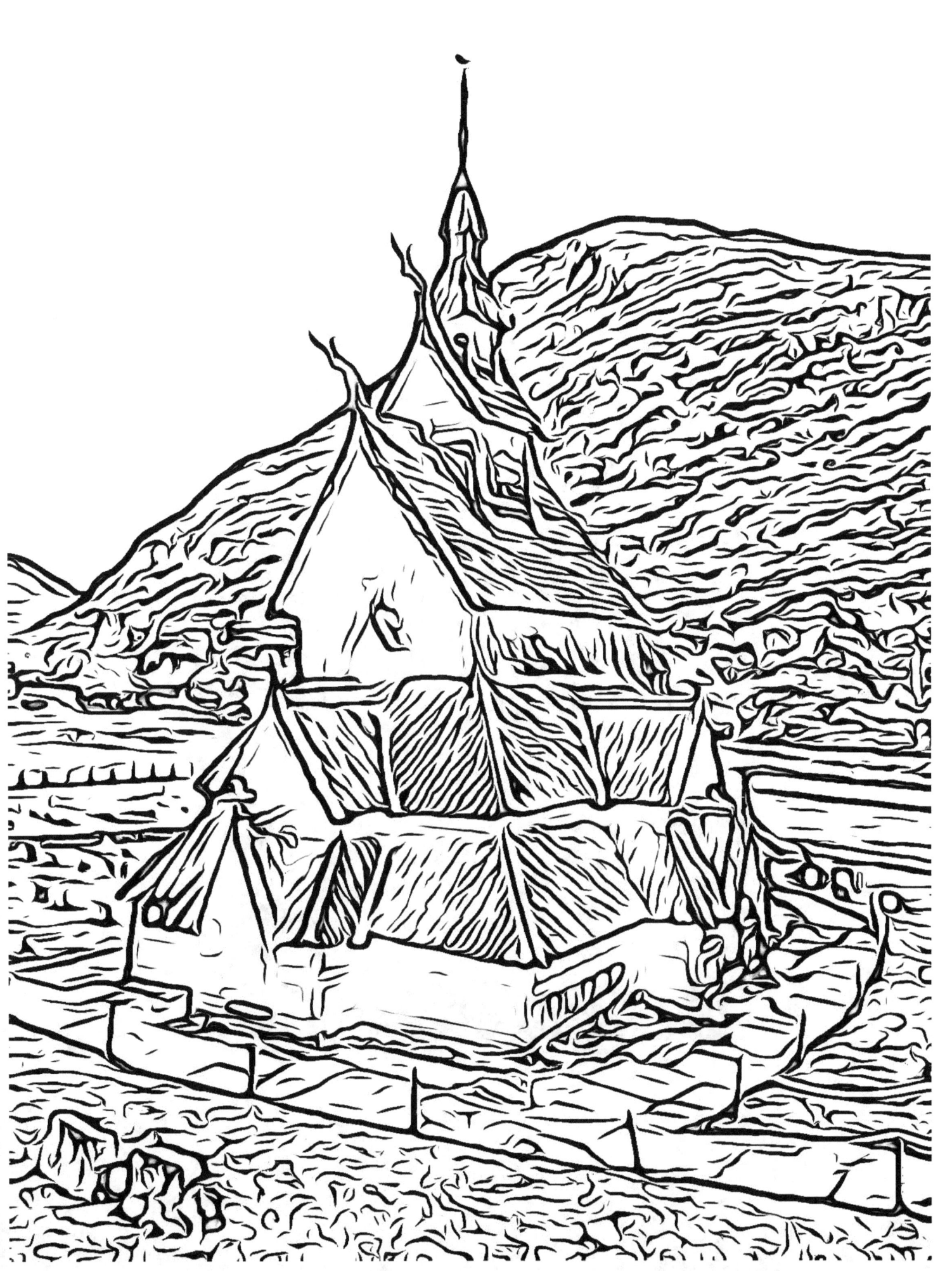

> Death does not
> concern us because
> as long as we exist
> death is not here
> and when it does come
> we no longer exist
> – Epicurus

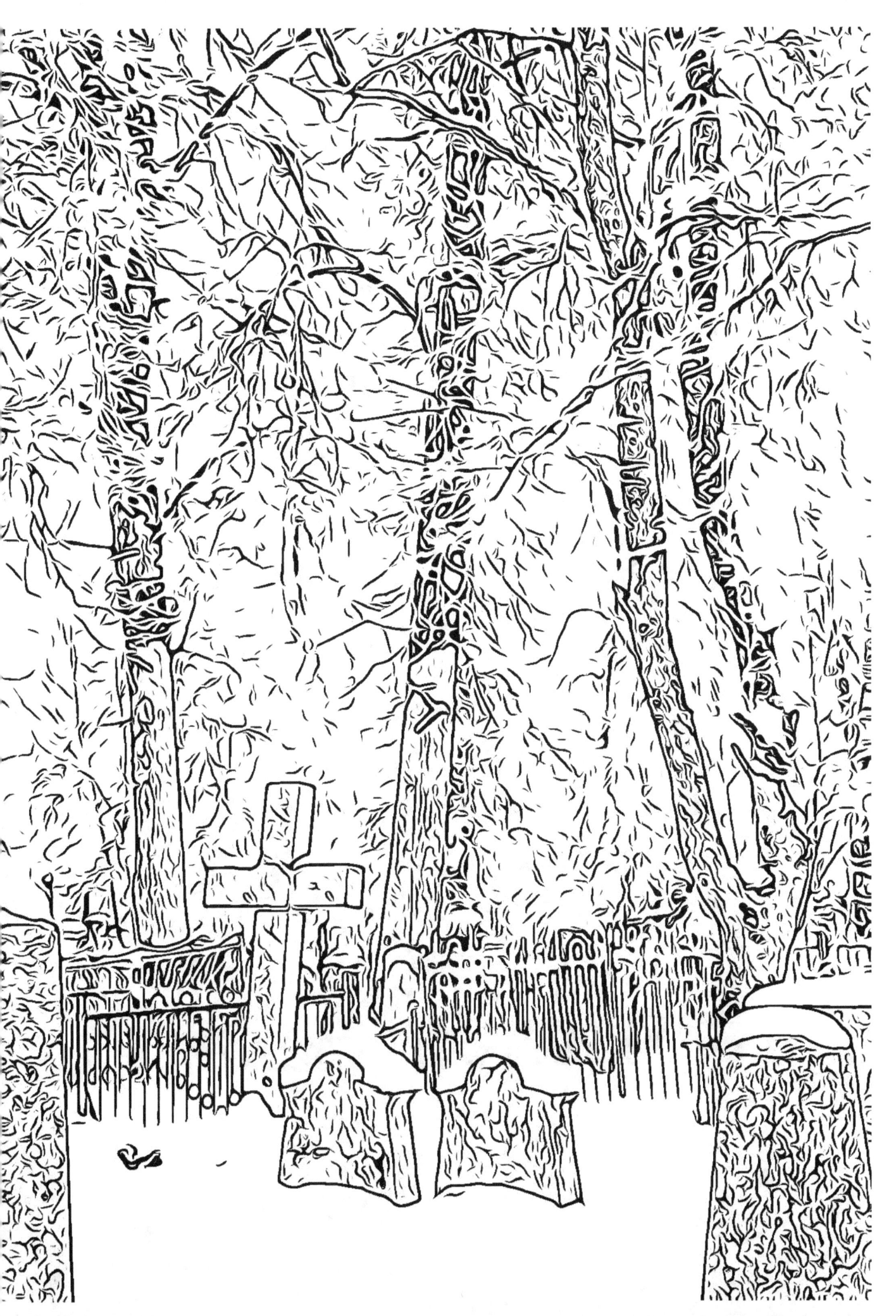

> They say you die twice
> One time when you stop
> breathing and a second
> time a bit later on
> when somebody says
> your name
> for the last time
>
> – Banksy

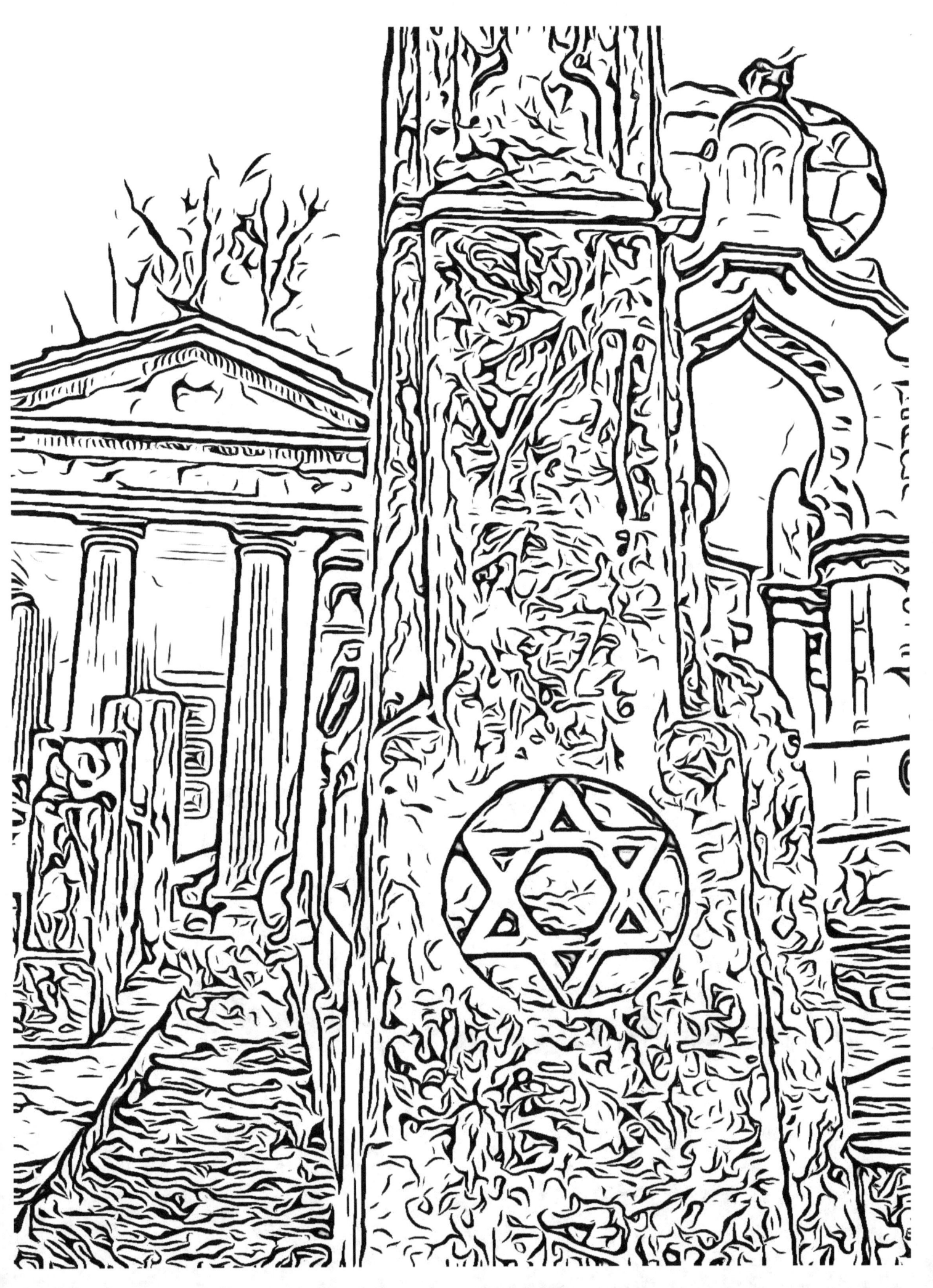

Death is
the wish
of some
the relief
of many
and the
end of all

— Lucius Annaeus Seneca

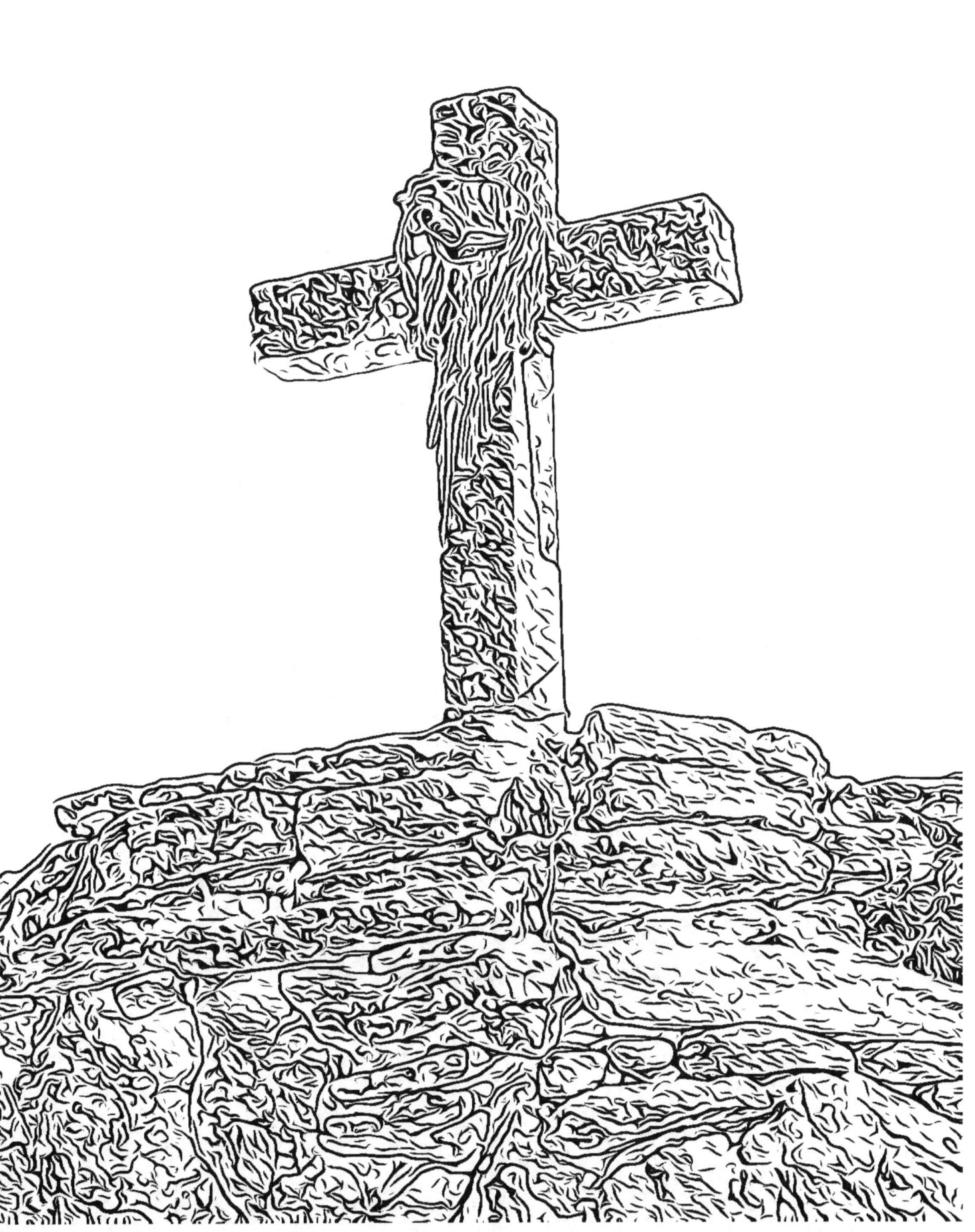

> Let life be
> beautiful like
> summer flowers
> and death
> like autumn leaves
>
> – Rabindranath Tagore

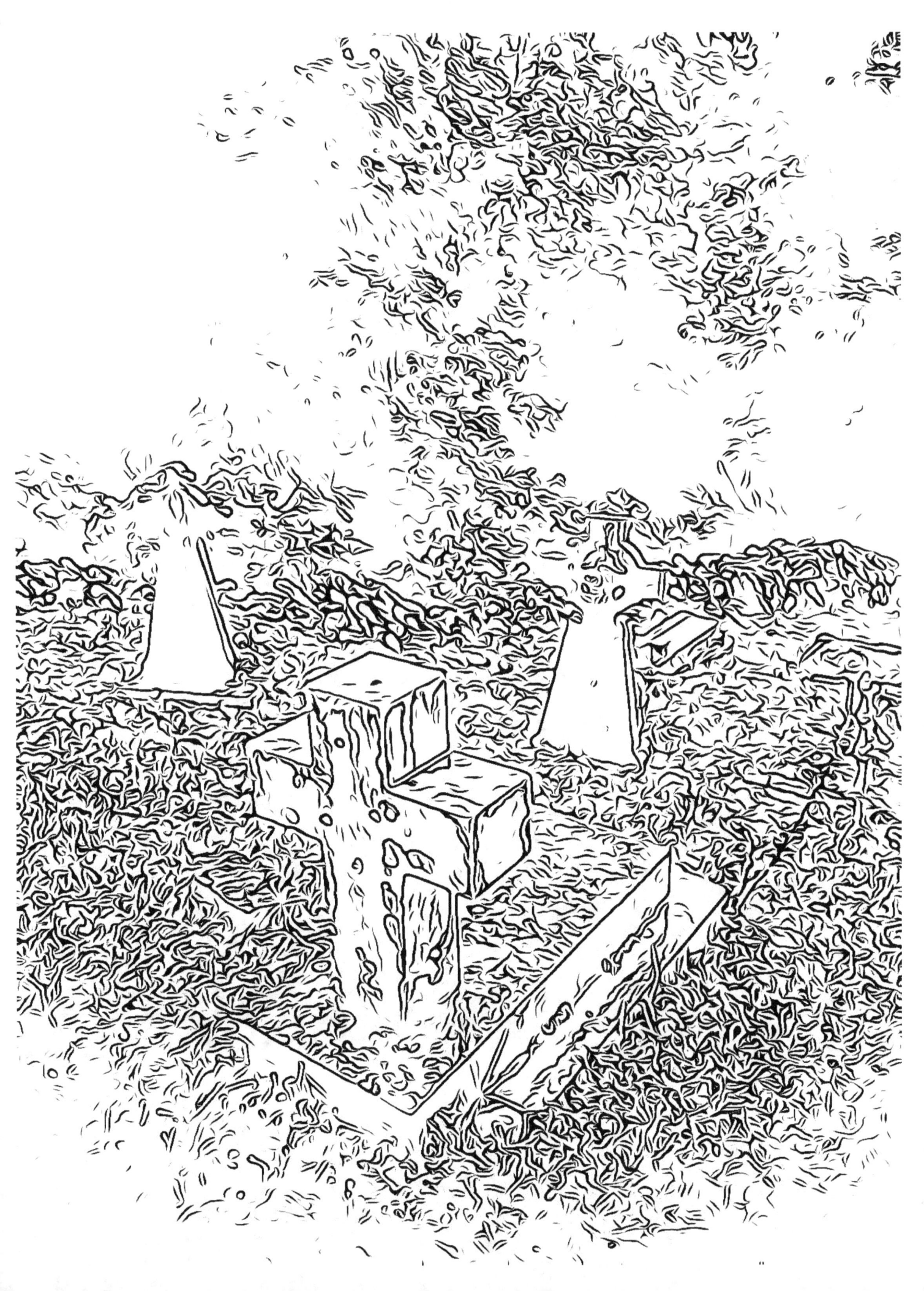

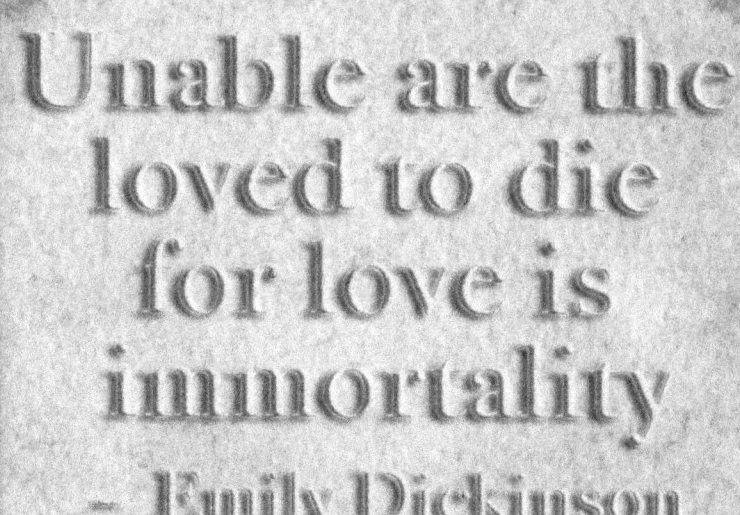

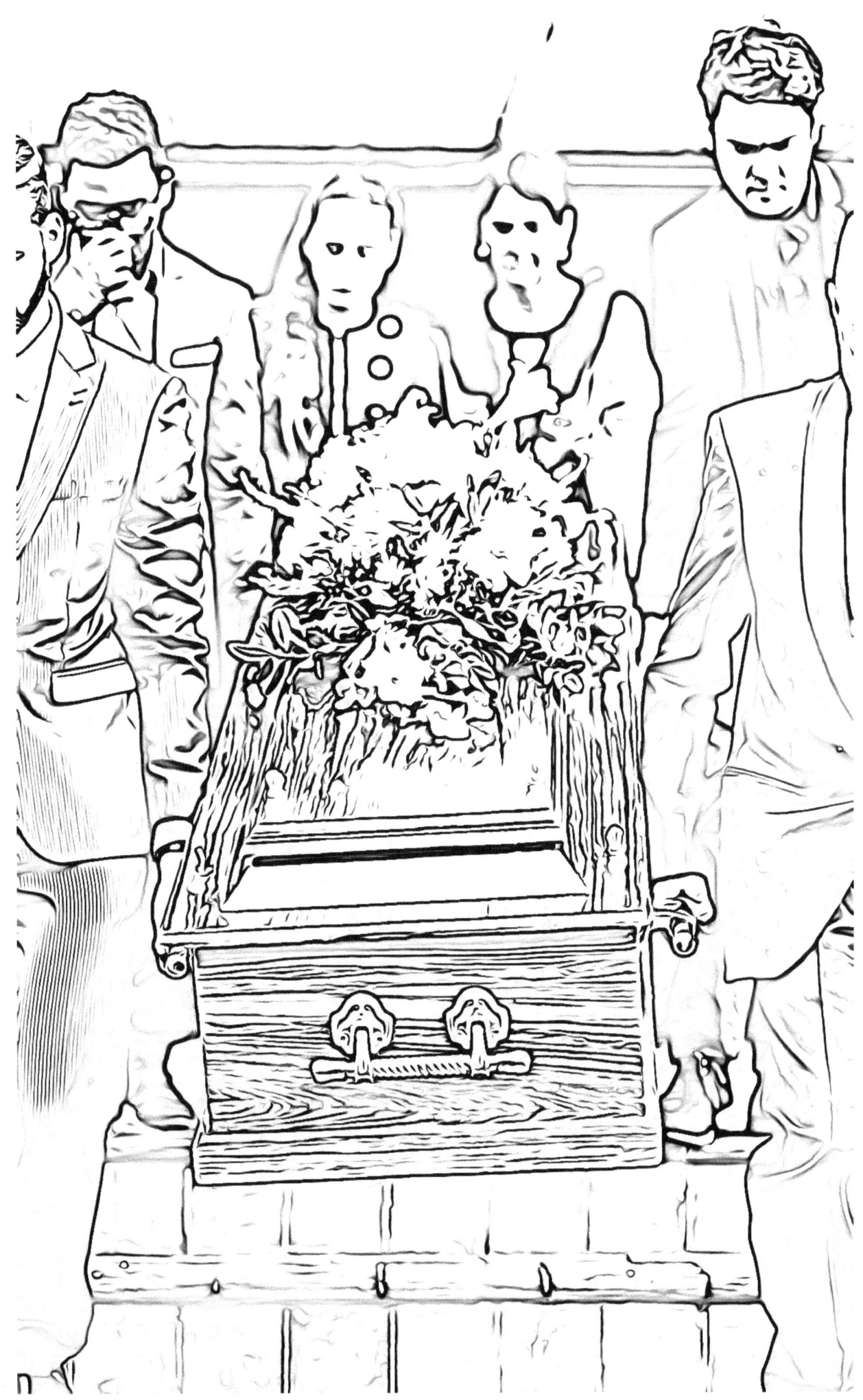

> Loss and possession
> death and life are one
> There falls no shadow
> where there shines
> no sun
> – Hilaire Belloc

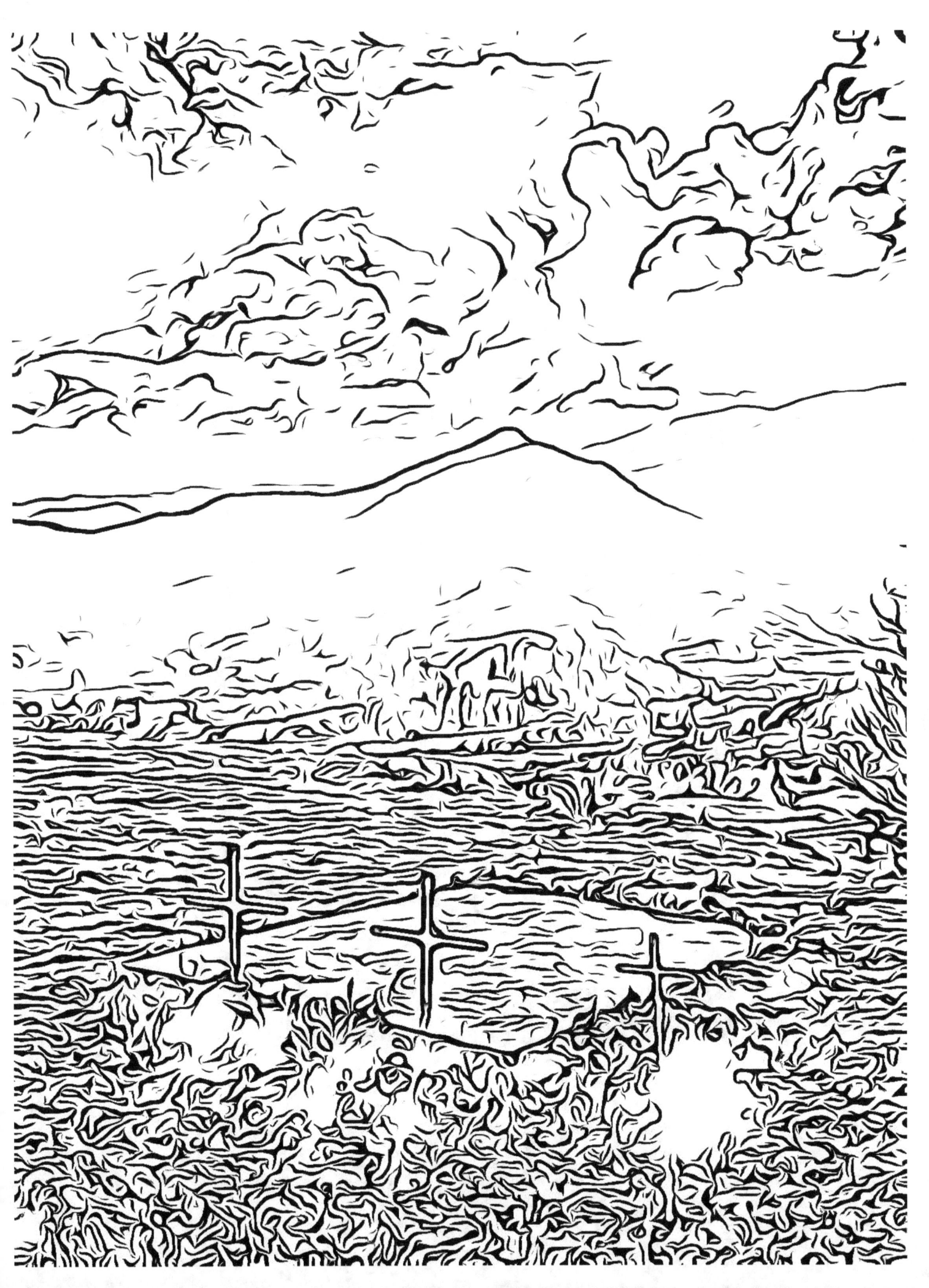

> Life is hard
> Then you die
> Then they throw
> dirt in your face
> Then the worms eat you
> Be grateful it happens
> in that order
>
> – David Gerrold

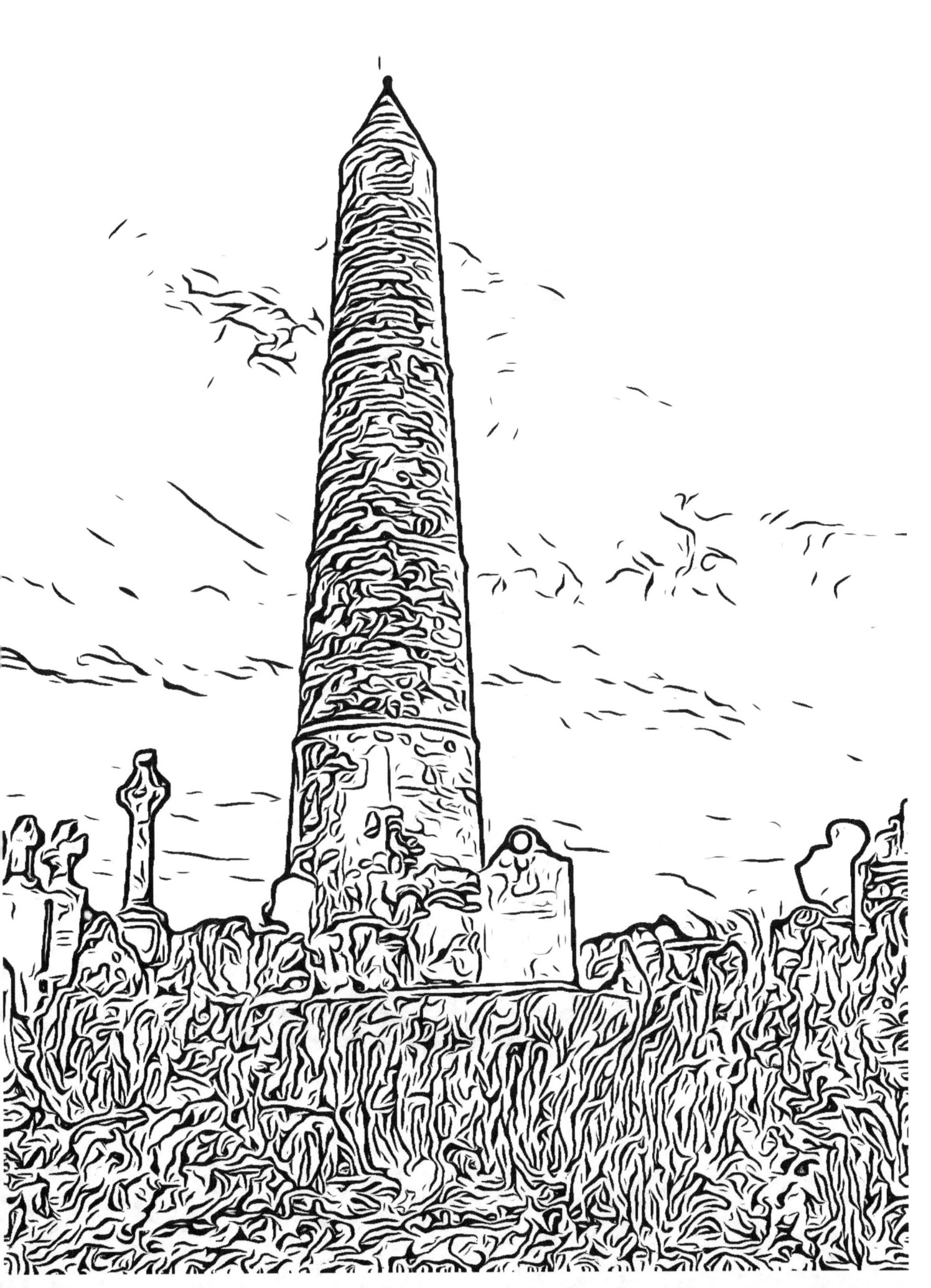

> The boundaries
> which divide
> Life from Death
> are at best shadowy
> and vague
> – Edgar Allan Poe

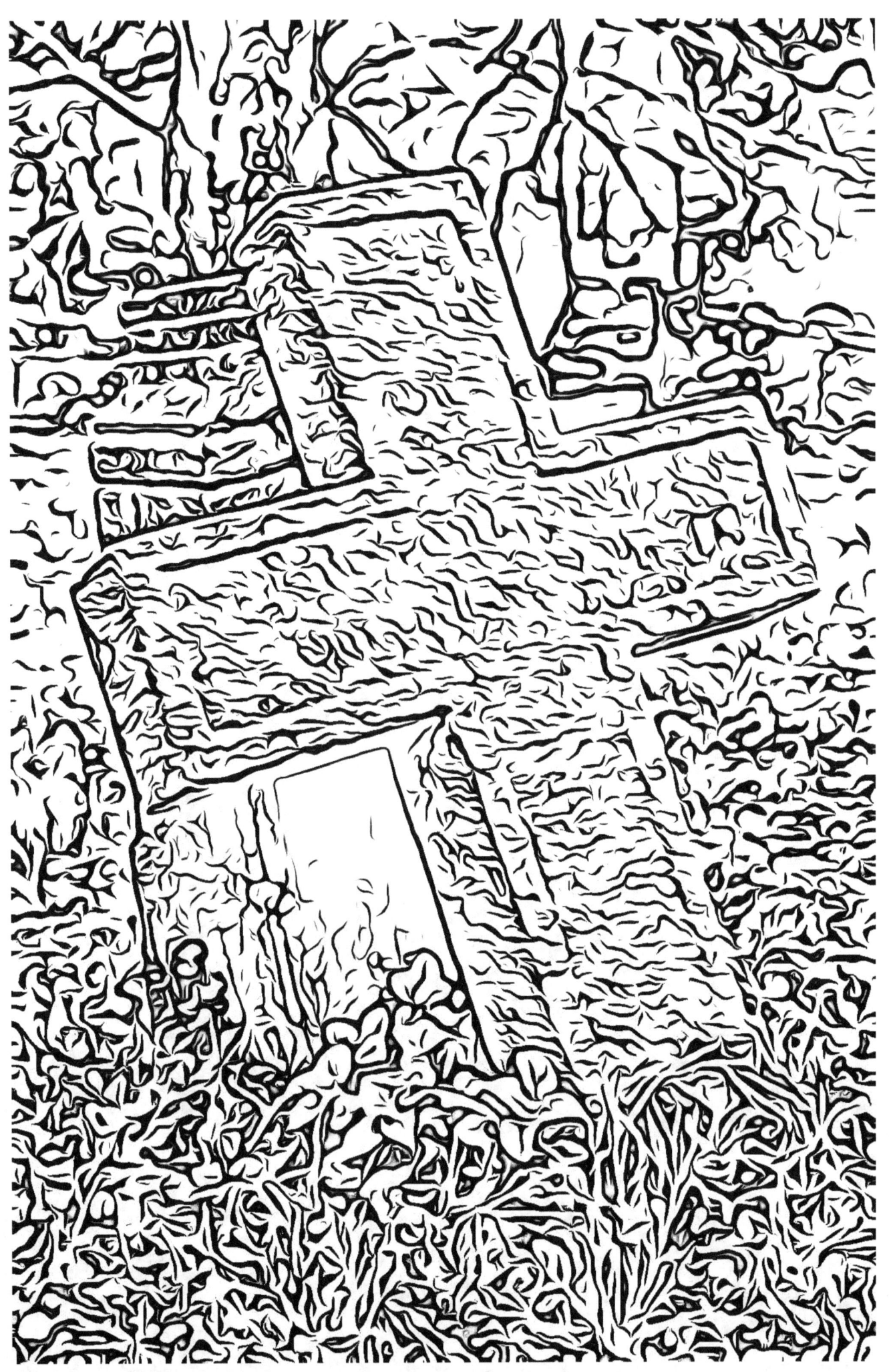

"The bitterest tears shed over graves are for words left unsaid and deeds left undone"

– Harriet Beecher-Stowe

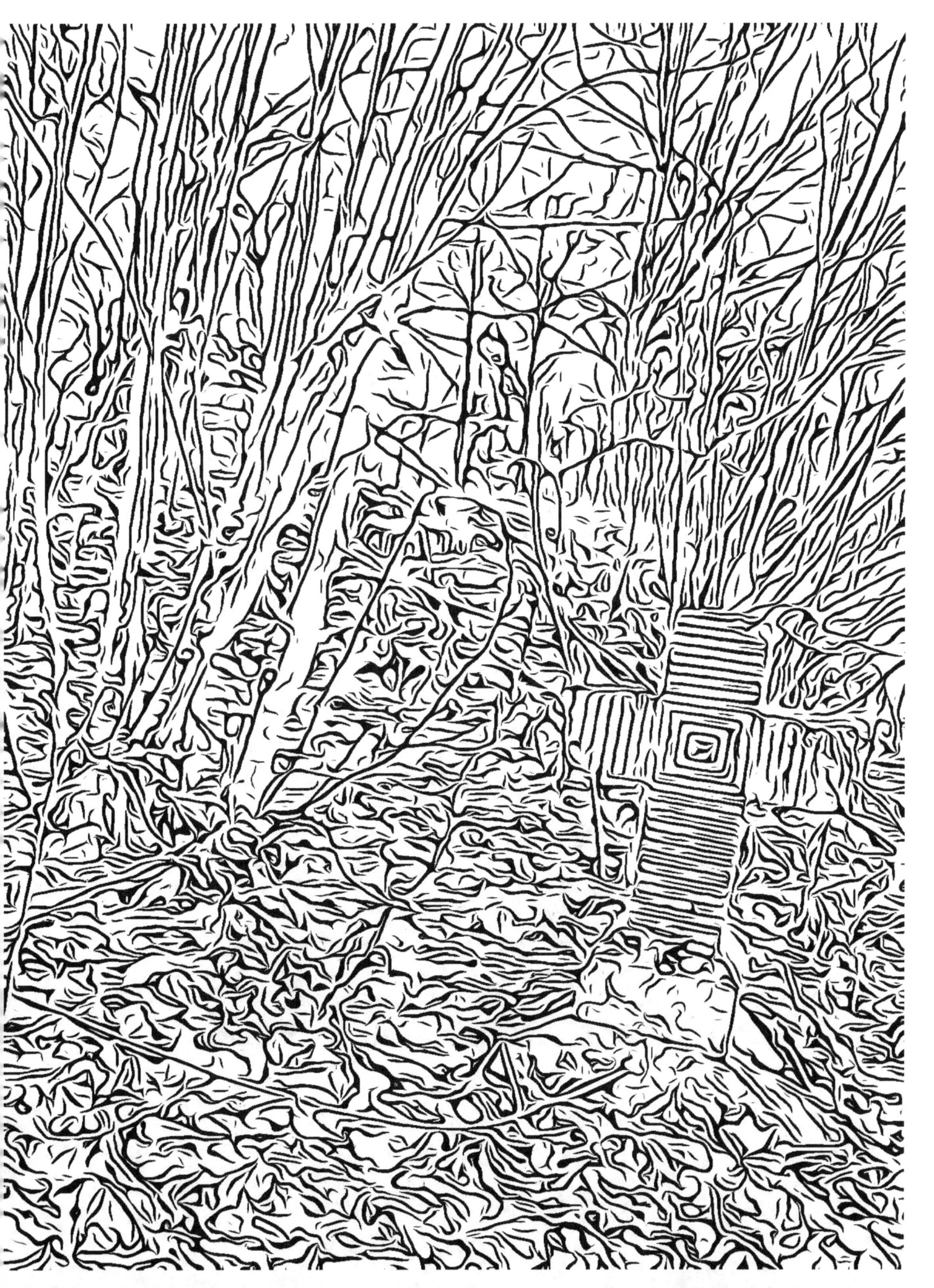

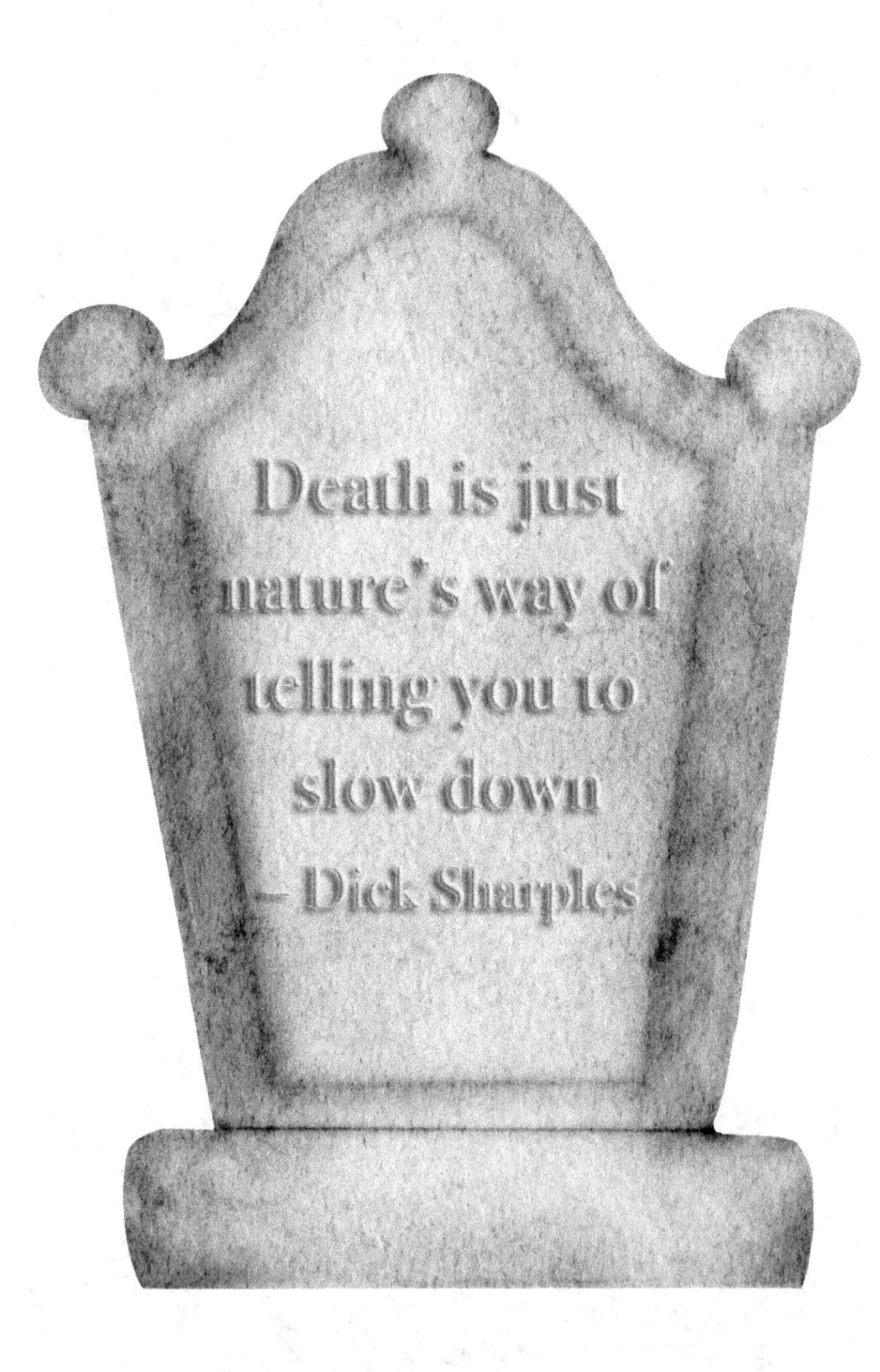

www.ingramcontent.com/pod-product-compliance
Lightning Source LLC
Chambersburg PA
CBHW060440220526
45465CB00008B/3211